MASTERING WUSHU

By
Jiang Bangjun & Emilio Alpanseque

EMPIRE Books
P.O. Box 491788, Los Angeles, CA 90049
www.empirebooks.net

Disclaimer
Please note that the author and publisher of this book are NOT RESPONSIBLE in any manner whatsoever for any injury that may result from practicing the techniques and/or following the instructions given within. Since the physical activities described herein may be too strenuous in nature for some readers to engage in safely, it is essential that a physician be consulted prior to training.

Copyright © 2007 by Empire Books

All rights reserved. No part of this publication may be reproduced or utilized in any form or by any means, electronic or mechanical, including photocopying, recording, or by any information storage and retrieval system, without prior written permission from Empire Books.

Empire Books
P.O. Box 491788
Los Angeles, CA 90049

First edition
07 06 05 04 03 02 01 00 99 98 1 3 5 7 9 10 8 6 4 2
Printed in the United States of America.

ISBN-10: 1-933901-31-4
ISBN-13: 978-1-933901-31-2

Library of Congress Cataloging-in-Publication Data

Jiang, Bangjun.
  Mastering wushu / by Jiang Bangjun & Emilio Alpanseque.
     p. cm.
  ISBN 978-1-933901-31-2 (pbk. : alk. paper)
  1. Martial arts. I. Alpanseque, Emilio. II. Title.
  GV1101.J53 2007
  796.815'5--dc22

2007011797

Cover photo courtesy of Jason Alan
Cover & text design: Mario M. Rodriguez, MMRDesign Solutions.

Wu (武) is the Chinese word for "war" or "martial". The Wu character is composed of Zhi (止), to stop, to cease, to end) and Ge (戈) spear, lance, weapons in general) and together with the chacacter Shu (术) methods, skills) they form the word Wushu. Consequently, it is said that ancient men could have defined Wushu as the "method to stop weapons" or "method for averting violence", thus reaching a state of tranquility where there is no conflict at all.

Calligraphy by Yang Shengbao
Renqiu City, Hebei Province, P.R. China.

Foreword by Coach Wu Bin

World-renowned Coach Wu Bin graduated from the Beijing University of Physical Education with a major in Wushu in 1963, and started working for the Beijing Wushu Institute thereafter. In 1970, after the foundation of the legendary Beijing Wushu Team, Coach Wu was assigned to organize a comprehensive plan in order to guarantee the team's later success. He recruited high potential athletes and coached them under a strict and scientific training system, producing more Wushu champions than any other coach in China, including the international movie star Jet Li. Today, after dedicating more than four decades to Wushu, Coach Wu Bin holds an official 9th degree, also called "Golden Dragon", the highest possible ranking of Wushu recognition.

Emilio and Bangjun,

I am very glad to know that the two of you have written in conjunction a book about the basic skills and elementary movements of Wushu Changquan. Currently there are many Wushu athletes around the world, including the United States. Some may practice Changquan and some may practice other styles of Wushu, however, regardless of the style, they certainly need to practice diligently the basic skills and elementary movements first, so they can advance to practice routines and fighting abilities.

The Practice of Changquan basic skills and elementary movements is the foundation for learning Changquan routines. Correct basic skills allow the athlete to perform and complete standard moves according to strict specifications. High quality basic skills allow the athlete to practice single movements and connections naturally and smoothly, understanding and showcasing the skills and effects of the relationships between hard and soft, quick and slow, as well as a strong sense of rhythm.

Changquan is a new term. It is the general denomination for Shaolinquan, Chaquan, Huaquan, Hongquan (Red), Hongquan (Flood), Fanziquan, Liuhequan, Mizongquan and other styles of Wushu. Therefore, the routines of Changquan must include movements from all these traditional styles. Furthermore, there are general characteristics know as the "four fighting methods", "eight qualities" and "twelve descriptions" that should be clearly demonstrated during the performance of a routine. For example, it shall have the power and strength of Shaolinquan, the flexibility and exquisite movement execution of Chaquan, the fluid long-range movements of Huaquan, etc. Lastly, during the practice of the basic skills and elementary movements, special attention shall be given to the different attack and defense applications of every movement to allow the learners to better grasp the speed, flexibility and stability of Changquan. Changquan is not only an exercise for competition or performance; it is also a good source for improving one's health, learning self-defense as well as practicing moral cultivation.

Wu Bin, Beijing, P.R. China. 2007

恩米
邦军：

  我很高兴你们合作出版了一本有关武术长拳的基本功和基本动作的一本书。现在世界上练习武术的人很多，美国也是如此。有练习长拳的，也有练习其他各个门派的武术。但是无论练习哪一种拳，一定要练好该门拳的基本功和基本动作，才能进一步练好套路以及交手的功夫。

  练习长拳基本功和基本动作是练习长拳套路的基础。正确的基本动作能完美的完成和表现动作的规格。高质量的基本功能使动作和动作连接更有协调性、连贯性，能在套路中更好地体现刚柔相济、快慢相间、节奏分配的演练技巧和效果。

  长拳是新名词，是少林拳、查拳、华拳、红（洪）拳、翻子拳、六合拳、迷踪拳等等的统称。所以长拳套路中所编排的动作，一定应该具有这些传统套路中的动作。而所表现的技术也应该是属于"四击"、"八法"、"十二型"中的技术要求和特点，如少林拳的刚猛有力，查拳的小巧灵活，华拳的舒展大方等。最后还要特别注意在练习基本功和基本动作时，要介绍动作攻防技术，才能更好引导学习者对长拳快速、灵活、沉稳的特点，领悟更深刻。长拳不仅仅是表演、比赛的套路，应该也是健身、防身的修身养性的好拳种。

中国北京。2007。

Dedication

It has been 27 years that I walk the Wushu road, through sunny and rainy days, but I haven't been alone through all those years as my father has been my instructor right from the beginning. Even when I was an only naughty boy, my father has started to nurture my interest in Wushu, to teach me the basics, and to take me visit Wushu masters. He has instructed and encouraged my practice ever since. My father is my first and strictest coach and audience. It's also my father, who encouraged me as a teenager to look for better training thousands of miles away from him. That 4-year training in that physical education school finally allowed me to become a professional Wushu athlete. My father has followed me, observed me, and instructed me through all my national competitions. After I was selected to the national professional team, I have experienced career downfalls many times, for instance, the repeated injuries almost killed my sporting career and my confidence. It's my father who has consistently encouraged me and walked me through the difficult times again and again. No matter what has happened, my father always stands behind me, tells me not to give up, and encourages me to go further. When I achieved my gold medals, it's always my father who reminds me with a clear mind that I still have a long way to go and I shall train harder to reach the next level. My father has supported me through each step I walked from nobody to a world champion.

I began as a teenager Wushu student who started training later than others at an unknown amateur school, then I entered a professional physical education university and grew up to be a national champion, and later a world champion. From my home town to the world championships awarding podium, every step of my life had my father's contribution and love. No matter where I go, I know I have my father's eyes on me, crossing oceans and mountains, full of encouragement, pride, care, and endless love.

This book is dedicated to my beloved father.

- Jiang Bangjun

Dedication

  在武术之路上风雨兼程 27 年，父亲始终如一是我的良师。从我还是懵懂好动的顽皮男孩，父亲就留心培养我的兴趣，开始训练我的基本功，带我寻访武术前辈启蒙。从此指导督促我练功，风雨无阻，是我最早和最严的教练和陪练。也是父亲，鼓励少年的我离家千里求学，四年体校训练，引导我走上专业运动员道路。还是父亲，在我奔赴全国各地参赛时，尽其所能追随观摩，悉心指点。在我入选专业队后，一次次由于受伤几乎终止运动员生涯，一次次遭遇事业低谷几乎前功尽弃，是父亲坚持不懈的鼓励与支持，扶持我度过一关再一关。不管发生什么，父亲始终站在我身后，告诉我，不要放弃，坚持走下去。在我取得优秀成绩时，是父亲冷静的眼神在对我说，前路正长正远，不可自满，再接再厉。

  我从一个起步已晚的习武少年成长为全国冠军，世界冠军，从名不见经传的业余体校走入专业体育大学，从家乡走向世界体坛，其中的每一步每一段，都有着父亲默默支持的身影，不以言表的心血付出。无论我走到哪里，我知道父亲的目光跨越千山万水，凝注在我身上，那目光中饱含着鼓励，骄傲，劝勉和无尽的爱。

  谨以此书，献给我挚爱的父亲。

  — 江邦军

Dedication

This book is dedicated to the loving memory of my grandmother Adela Cordero, who always believed in me and never let me down through the hardships of raising me. In fact, as fate had it, it was her who accepted such responsibility without the slightest hesitation, demonstrating both her great courage and unconditional love for me. Although she was never directly involved on my decisions towards Wushu, her lessons on discipline, perseverance, patience and fair play helped me tremendously throughout my career. Today, I am sure that wherever she is, she is watching my every move with a smile and keeping me safe.

El presente libro está dedicado a la memoria de mi querida abuela Adela Cordero, quien siempre creyó en mí y nunca me abandonó durante la difícil tarea de criarme. De hecho, tal y como el destino lo tenía, fue ella quien aceptó tal responsabilidad sin el menor titubeo, demostrando tanto su gran valentía como su amor incondicional hacia mí. Aunque ella nunca estuvo directamente involucrada en mis decisiones con respecto al Wushu, sus lecciones sobre disciplina, perseverancia, paciencia y honestidad me ayudaron tremendamente a lo largo de mi carrera. Hoy, estoy seguro que donde sea que se encuentre, ella está siguiendo cada uno de mis movimientos con una sonrisa y manteniéndome a salvo.

- Emilio Alpanseque

Acknowledgments

First and foremost, we would like to thank all our Wushu mentors, past and present. This project has become a reality mainly on account of their genuine care about our development and success, not only as Wushu athletes, but as individuals. Our most sincere appreciation goes to them.

We would also like to thank many friends and colleagues who contributed to this book in one way or another. It is impossible to list them all, but particular thanks go to Matt Wong, Joe Scarcella, Viet Le, Peter Bandonis and Luciano Cassarino. Among the others who contributed importantly to bringing this book into being, we must express our gratitude to the folks at Empire Media for giving us the opportunity to publish our work with the flexibility we needed. Thanks to Jose M. Fraguas and Val Mijailovic for their excellent guidance as the project was moving along.

The main photography of this book was handled greatly by Jason Alan. Other photo credits go to Jose Vicente Serra, Enrique Amador and Peter Bandonis. The outstanding Chinese calligraphy art that opens the book was provided by Yang Shengbao. The Terracotta Army photo that leads the first chapter was taken at the Forbidden Gardens, a fascinating outdoor museum that replicates some of China's major historic scenes in Katy, Texas.

Lastly, we want to thank you, the reader, for letting us try to guide you on your own Wushu journey and allow the art of Wushu to transcend from one generation to another. Thanks to all!

Introduction

Wushu is an integral part of Chinese cultural heritage, a product of several millennia of development that combines martial arts, health preserving exercises, performance and sportive activities, and many more elements. Wushu originated at the dawn of human history, developed and evolved continuously adapting to the circumstances of each period of time. Today, Wushu, usually referred as Contemporary or Modern Wushu, has specialized into many different areas, one of them being a modern high level competitive sport that is slowly taking the world by storm.

Roughly speaking, Wushu competition is classified into two main categories: Taolu (Routines) and Sanda (Free Sparring). Taolu competition involves the performance of sequences of movements that represent the attack and defense techniques of Wushu and are divided into four main groups which are: Empty Hand, Weapons, Sparring Sets and Group Routines. Sanda competition consists of a full contact free sparring bout on top of a raised platform. As any other sport, Wushu competition has judging methods and scoring criteria stipulated by the International Wushu Federation, which is the main international governing body of the sport, founded in 1990 in Beijing, China.

When Wushu first began its internationalization process in the early 1980s, information about the foundation of the sport and its training methods was very limited outside of China. During those years, aspiring Wushu athletes from around the world had very limited sources to learn their craft. They had to consider themselves lucky if the could find some magazine articles or a copy of the very few manuals or books that were out, mostly written in Chinese language. Western students had to learn by improvising or adapting training methods of traditional martial arts or other sports, and in any other imaginable way. Unfortunately, despite their great efforts and enthusiasm, the results were far from being satisfactory. It is a fact that without a qualified instructor, correct methodology and the right sources of information, the process of learning Wushu effectively is almost impossible.

As time progressed, very few countries were fortunate enough to have qualified coaches from China, the United States and Canada were perhaps two of the very rare exceptions due to their big Chinese settlements; however, the vast majority of countries around the world did not have coaches or any other source of information. Next, as China started to organize International Wushu Festivals, the first foreign delegations started to have access to learn and compete with the very best. Anyone from that generation will be able to remember the true value of having a third or fourth generation copy of a personal videotape of a Chinese competition or a training session of a Chinese provincial team; for many, that blurry footage was the closest thing to having a real coach for many years and hence the only way to develop Wushu in their countries.

During the 1990's, Wushu already had gained considerable international popularity, there were first generation foreign competitors acting as coaches in their original countries, at the same time, there were a few more Chinese coaches who had emigrated to a bigger selection of countries around the world, but for some reason the sources of quality information continued to be very scarce, especially in other languages than Chinese. Notice that language has always been a major

obstacle to learning Wushu efficiently. The best Chinese Wushu coaches usually only speak Chinese and Chinese is a very difficult language for Foreign Wushu athletes to learn. And even though China has published series of Wushu textbooks in English, some of the translations were far from being adequate and the contents too rudimentary. Furthermore, the books were not always up to date and were only illustrated by a limited number of drawings, which failed to transmit the nature of the movements clearly. In fact, there was an evident lack of standardization of Wushu terminology and training methodology as well.

Today, Wushu has become a global phenomenon with tremendous cross-over appeal. Wushu can be seen in western movies, TV programs, advertisements and all kinds of other media. The sport of Wushu is being practiced officially in more than one hundred and eleven countries around the world, with a possibility of being introduced into the Olympics; but still, we wholeheartedly believe that the availability of good sources of information has not improved significantly. Therefore, the necessity of compiling a comprehensive and authoritative material on Wushu became overwhelming for us and eventually decided to embark on this project enthusiastically, as we felt ready to share our knowledge and experience with our readers. This was, quite obviously, a very challenging task, but we have worked very hard upon making it happen.

Welcome to MASTERING WUSHU! Finally a well produced instructional book that encompasses all fundamental skills, training principles and terminology of Wushu is available in a convenient single volume in English language. The book starts off with a foreword written by Coach Wu Bin, one of the most respected Wushu coaches around the world, discussing several basic concepts and definitions that are essential to understanding Modern Wushu. After that, the first chapter does a great job narrating the complete history of Wushu in a way we believe has never been accomplished before. The second chapter covers all the most important Wushu basic skills and elementary movements divided in: Stretching and Flexibility Exercises, Hand Forms and Hand Techniques, Stances and Footwork, Basic Combinations, Balance Techniques, Jumping Techniques and Tumbling Techniques. The third chapter meticulously covers a Basic Compulsory Routine and an appendix has been included with all the technical terminology written in English, in Chinese simplified characters and romanized following the Pinyin transcription method.

From the original concept and proposal to the final book, MASTERING WUSHU was a lot more work than we originally anticipated, but our efforts could not end with the book, we have gone further and also produced a DVD in order to make a clear difference and radically enhance your learning experience. The DVD includes a complete presentation of all the techniques and training principles presented in the book plus whole new sections on Advanced Warm-up Exercises, Advanced Conditioning and Strengthening Exercises, and a totally new and never before seen Advanced Competition Personal Routine by Jiang Bangjun. We are convinced that having both the book and the DVD is the best way to present this material, as one complements the other. With the book, you can read the descriptions and look at the photographs, and on the other hand, with the DVD you can see an exact demonstration of the each exercise exactly how it should be done. It is a great advantage and definitely unprecedented in terms of the Wushu publications available until today.

Learning fundamentals while developing coordination, flexibility and strength are the keys for success in all sports. And there is no reason to assume that Wushu is any different. By learning the most current Wushu basic techniques, practitioners develop a foundation allowing them to go as far in Wushu as their ability and interest allows. Emphasis should always be placed on correct form and technique to reduce injuries, ensure against bad habits that might restrict your Wushu potential in later years and promote learning safely and efficiently. Invariably, whether you are a beginner, an experienced competitor or a coach, these two products are a must for your collection. MASTERING WUSHU is by far your best first step into Wushu excellence! Good Luck!

Mastering Wushu

Table of Contents

1 Wushu History ——— Page 2
1.1. Prehistoric Era
(Prior to 2100 B.C.)
1.2. Ancient Era
(2100 B.C. - 221 B.C.)
1.3. Imperial Era
(221 B.C. - 1912)
1.4. Modern Era (1912 - Present)

2 Wushu Basic Training ——— Page 17
2.1. Stretching and Flexibility Training
2.2. Hand Forms and Hand Techniques
2.3. Stances and Footwork
2.4. Leg Techniques
2.5. Basic Combinations
2.6. Balance Techniques
2.7. Jumping Techniques

3 Wushu Basic Routine ——— Page 97
3.1. Opening Movement
3.2. Section One
3.3. Section Two
3.4. Section Three
3.5. Section Four
3.6. Closing Movement

4 Appendixes ——— Page 123
4.1. Bibliographical References
4.2. About the Authors
4.3. Glossary of Terms

XIV

Mastering Wushu

Chapter 1

Wushu History

The Terracotta Army is one of the most significant archeological excavations of the 20th century. Over 7000 life size terracotta figures of warriors and horses arranged in battle formations are replicas of what the imperial army should look like in those days of pomp and vigor.

Introduction

China is well known as an ancient civilization with a recorded history of nearly 4,000 years. Because of its length and complexity, the history of Wushu lends itself to the most diverse interpretations as well. Despite these essential drawbacks, there have been important works of research performed by eminent scholars that range from old-timers like Tang Hao (1897-1959), generally regarded the first true historian of Chinese martial arts, to contemporary ones such as Ma Mingda (1943-) or Kang Gewu (1948-). Without a doubt, the records collected by these authors are priceless contributions that now constitute not only an important source of information, but also a significant connection to China's past.

On this section, we humbly attempt to present a synthesis and chronology of the history of Chinese martial arts based on many of the aforementioned sources. We have tried to approach this arduous task by splitting it into four phases: Prehistoric Era (prior to 2100 B.C.), Ancient Era (2100 B.C. - 221 B.C.), Imperial Era (221 B.C. - 1912) and Modern Era (1912 - Present). Subsequently, we have selected some of the most relevant milestones, trying to outline those traditions that are immediately linked to today's Wushu. Readers will find that the most important cluster of information is contained on the last section, which describes in full detail the development of Wushu from the moment the last imperial dynasty was overthrown until today.

As it is often said, knowing our past may enable us to understand our present and perhaps even change our future. We anticipate that the information presented on this chapter will clarify many hidden aspects of Wushu by spreading awareness about its history and position within Chinese culture. Hopefully, it will also open doors for further research into these subjects by others.

1.1. Prehistoric Era (Prior to 2100 B.C.)

Wushu has undergone a long process of evolution that predates recorded history, therefore we cannot really trace the exact time when Wushu could have started. So far, the earliest primitive human discovered in China, known as the Yuanmou Man, lived roughly 1.7 million years ago. Subsequently, there was the Lantian Man who lived about 1,000,000 to 600,000 years ago, and the Beijing Man, who lived about 500,000 to 200,000 years ago. It is safe to assume that primitive forms of martial skills could have evolved directly from the hunting and self-preservation needs of these early men as they were forced to develop the ability to defend against animals and other men as means of subsistence. The Beijing Man, for instance, was able to walk upright, make simple tools from bones and wood by using rocks and knew how to start fire. Most likely, as these early men divided into clans or tribes and conflicts would arise, gradually the first productive methods for attack employing arms, legs and the most basic weapons were developed, setting the starting point for the martial arts that we have today.

1.2. Ancient Era (2100 B.C. - 221 B.C.)

According to Chinese historians, the Xia Dynasty (2100 B.C. - 1766 B.C.) marked the end of prehistory. It has been uncovered that during this period, the ruling families developed weapons from rocks and started to work with bronze. Later, during the Shang Dynasty (1766 B.C. - 1027 B.C.), Chinese mastered the technology of smelting bronze and new weapons emerged such as the dagger-axe, the spear, etc. Embryonic forms of military exercises such as the "Dance of Axe and Shield" and the "Head Butting with Horns" belonged to this era. By the time of the Western Zhou Dynasty (1027 B.C. - 771 B.C.) specific military and civilian Wushu activities such as archery, swordsmanship, weightlifting and a variety of wrestling skills were well established. During the Spring and Autumn period (770 B.C. - 476 B.C.) followed by the Warring States period (475 B.C. - 221 B.C.) the country was divided in many small and big kingdoms which constantly warred with each other.

However, in this turbulent time many different philosophies known as the "Hundred Schools of Thought" flourished in order to provide strategic and political ideologies to strengthen the state, increase its military prowess and improve the preparation of their elite officials. Confucianism, Daoism, Legalism and others like Yin and Yang, Five Elements or Militarism are amongst the most important ones. In regards of Wushu, the effect of the combined work of such schools, both immediately and over the millennia, will also have an effect on the armed and unarmed systems of that period. For instance, as early as the year 500 B.C., famous philosopher Confucius taught his students six different subjects for scholarship including archery and charioting, that fall into the domain of Wushu. Furthermore, the importance of integrating the principles of the Yin and Yang, the unity between internal and external practices, the control of breathing, mind and spirit were already mentioned by Yue Nu, a legendary female warrior from the Yue Kingdom, according to the classic "Annals of Springs and Autumns of Wu and Yue". The School of Militarism, lead by Sun Zi, Wu Qi, Sun Bin and others military experts, produced various important military strategy manuals and philosophical texts, including the famous "The Art of War" by Sun Zi, perhaps the most influential and oldest treatise on military tactics in the world. Sun Zi's teachings, though originally studied within the context of larger wars, later would become fundamental principles of combat systems for soldiers and civilians. The Warring States Period came to an end when the military strongest state, the Qin, gained control over the entire area in 221 B.C. indicating the beginning of imperial China.

1.3. Imperial Era (221 B.C. - 1912)

Once the Qin Dynasty (221 B.C. - 206 B.C.) was consolidated, the unification of what we know today as China commenced. Their leader proclaimed himself the First Emperor of Qin, or Qin Shi Huangdi and during his reign, he standardized the language, the writing, the units of measure, the currency, and so forth. Two of his most important achievements are his involvement with the building of the Great Wall of China and the construction of his own tomb, a magnificent mausoleum that included over 7,000 pottery soldiers, weapons, chariots and even horses known as the Terracotta Army. The tomb was accidentally discovered in 1974, and priceless information about the distribution and formation of the soldiers, the use of weapons and the application of military tactics in those days has been studied since then.

After the civil war that followed the death of Qin Shihuangdi in 210 B.C., the Han Dynasty (206 B.C. - 220 A.D.) emerged, notable also for its military prowess. During this period, the importance of cavalry decreased the use of short weapons and new long weapons were developed such as long-handled broadsword, long halberd, single hook spears and more. The Han Dynasty also provides the first examples of early forms of health promotion exercises. In 1973, a scroll that dates back to the Western Han (206 B.C. - 9 A.D.) was unearthed which depicted the early med-

Illustration of the Terracotta Army

ical exercises of Daoyin. Also, near the end of the Eastern Han (A.D. 25 - 220), a renowned medical doctor named Hua Tuo created a set of exercises called Wuqinxi (Five Animal Play), mimicking the movements of the bear, tiger, deer, monkey and crane to circulation of Qi inside the human body. After the Han dynasty, there were nearly four centuries of turbulence, civil wars and disunity in China. The country split and unified several times, there were many kings, different armies and different geographic locations, therefore Wushu developed at many different levels.

During the Northern Wei Dynasty (386 - 534), in the year 495, the legendary Shaolin Temple was built in the Henan Province nestled in the foothills of the mount Song. According to historical records, at the end of the Sui Dynasty (581 - 618), Shaolin monks played a significant military role saving Tang army general Li Shimin from the enemy, which aided the establishment of the Tang Dynasty. This rescue may have caused the emergence of an army of "fighting monks" at the temple that would remain active for many years, learning combat methods from military experts as well as developing their own. The Wushu of Shaolin, or Shaolinquan, is one of the most famous styles of Wushu around the world. Hundreds of pages have been written, countless movies and TV series produced based upon the story about an Indian monk by the name of Bodhidharma ("Putidamo" or simply "Damo" in Chinese) setting the seeds for it, however, several historians have proven this to be mostly false. The Wushu of Shaolin is in fact an amalgamation of Wushu techniques and styles practiced in that area by secular Wushu masters, monks and army soldiers during several centuries.

During the Tang Dynasty (618 - 907), unprecedented developments in the fields of politics, economics, military power and culture were achieved. Li Shimin continued to lead the army and later became Emperor Taizong and set about reforming and unifying China. In terms of Wushu, Li Shimin is known for developing both military and civilian approaches according to different times and circumstances. For instance, he created a professional army and adapted the imperial examination system to be used for selecting the best soldiers. He also granted land and funding to the Shaolin Temple, appointing some of its monks as high-ranking military officers, etc. Later, as military conflicts became a thing of the past, Li Shimin gathered musicians, choreographers and Wushu experts to compose spectacular Martial Dances and Sword Dances as a way to commemorate military culture among soldiers and civilians during times of peace. Consequently, the standards for performance Wushu developed rapidly during this period, also considered the zenith of performing arts in China.

In 907, after more than a decade of steep decline, the one magnificent Tang Dynasty inevitably came to an end followed by a period of warfare and fragmentation known as the Five Dynasties and Ten Kingdoms (907-960), which torn the country apart for half a century. Upon the invention of gunpowder, traditional Wushu weapons such as swords, lances and bows were classified as "cold" weapons" as the first "fire" weapons, mostly flying fireballs and grenades, were employed in military warfare. These new fire weapons added defensive strength to the armies but cold weapons continued to be dominant as the armies issued standards for Wushu practice among the soldiers that included strength training, wrestling, swordsmanship, cavalry and more.

In 960, famous General Zhao Kuangyin established the Song Dynasty (960-1279) reunifying the country one more time under one single empire, and thus becoming Emperor Taizu of Song. It is believed that Emperor Taizu created a fighting style known as Taizu Changquan (Long-range Boxing of Taizu) based on his superior martial skills, allegedly obtained after studying in the

Segment of one the ancient murals at the Shaolin Temple

Shaolin Temple. The famous term "Eighteen Military Weapons" was already in use during the Song Dynasty. The term commonly refers to nine short weapons and nine long ones, but in reality Wushu weapons were never restricted to only eighteen. This is only a generic name used both in military text books as well as classic novels. Another famous hero of this period was General Yue Fei, who won brilliant victories recovering most part of the territory. Many important styles of Wushu like Chuojiao (Poking Feet), Fanzi (Flapping Fists), Xingyiquan (Form and Will Boxing) and Yingzhao (Eagle Claw) have been attributed to him.

By the mid-thirteenth century, the Mongols dominated the Song and established the first foreign dynasty to rule all China, the Yuan Dynasty (1271-1368). Historical records demonstrate that during this period military Wushu continued to be very important within the armies. It is said that Mongol warriors carried at least a broadsword, a spear with a small hook in the base of the blade and two versions of bows. It is also known that their training included the Three Male Sports: Horsemanship, archery, and wrestling. Actually, Mongolian wrestling is reputed to have influenced Chinese Wushu in general with its powerful control techniques and takedowns. In addition, the Shaolin Temple may have branched out into many other locations such as Luoyan and Taiyuan during this era. Besides the advances on military Wushu, many developments were achieved in the field of civilian Wushu. Traditional operas made extensive use of Wushu skills as they recreated great battles, with actors engaging in full fight scenes, brandishing fake weapons and performing stylized forms of combat movements. Consequently, a new branch of performance Wushu, or "Huafa Wuyi" (Entertainment Martial Arts) would become a separate entity from "Shizhan Wuyi" (War Martial Arts) and continue to be present up to the creation of the Beijing Opera during the late 1800s.

Mongol rule in China was brought to an end as the Ming Dynasty (1368-1644) was established, reuniting China one more time through a period of cultural restoration and expansion. The Ming Dynasty is also known as the golden era for military Wushu due to noticeable advances in many important areas. According to historical records, by the latter half of the Ming Dynasty classifications of codified systems of Wushu became recognizable styles. General Qi Jiguang, another hero of China, wrote a book called the "New Book of Effective Discipline", which is truly a masterpiece dedicated to many aspects of "Military Training" and "Military Strategy. This book was written around 1560 and has several chapters dedicated to Wushu. Taizu Changquan (Long-range Boxing of Taizu), Duanquan (Short-range Boxing), Fanziquan (Flapping Fists), Houquan (Monkey Boxing), staff techniques learned from General You Dayou, spear techniques of the Yang and Ma families, and many other martial arts systems are mentioned. General Qi also expressed his opposition to "flowery fists and embroidered legs", referring to martial art forms that lack practical usage, and developed a method of 32 techniques which were a synthesis of the 16 different styles that he had studied; which some identify as on of the possible origins of Taijiquan (Tai Chi).

Historical records from this era point out that the Shaolin Temple became a focal point for martial arts. For example, previously mentioned General You Dayou taught his famous staff techniques to several monks who later passed his traditions down to others in the temple, and like him many others followed. There are precious ancient murals in the temple from this period that clearly depict monks engaged in Wushu practices. Military accounts from this period indicate that armies of monks from several temples, including Shaolin, took part in at least four military campaigns against Japanese pirates and other formidable foreign invaders – the Manchu – who conquered Beijing and established the Qing Dynasty (1644-1911) after many battles.

The new ruling class gradually controlled the whole country and banned the practice of all kinds of martial arts by civilians during the reign of Emperor Yongzheng (1723-1736). The Shaolin Temple was accused to cover anti-Qing revels inside its doors and eventually was burned down, forcing its survivors to migrate to the southern provinces of China other countries of South Asia. However, despite the strong opposition from the rulers, martial artists from different circles, including Shaolin, organized in activities of underground societies who continue to practice and develop Wushu for many decades. Perhaps based on the motto "To overthrow the Qing and return the Ming", many traditional Wushu styles such as Hongquan (Hung Gar), Yongchun (Wing Chun) and others evolved during this period. Moreover, during the last part of the XVIII century, several masters reinforced their styles by combining and assimilating the essence of several Chinese philosophies and medicine theories with their attack and defense skills, forging some of the most popular internal styles known today.

Unfortunately, upheaval and turmoil continued to shake the country throughout the whole XIX century, there were many revolutions and uprisings such as the Eight Trigrams Rebellion (1813), the Opium Wars (1839-1842 and 1856-1860), the Taiping Rebellion (1851-1864) and many more, which weakened China terribly. In addition, foreign forces also advanced into Chinese land defeating entire armies with their western weapons, which essentially vanished completely the use of Wushu for military purposes, other than improving the physical condition of the soldiers. Terrible events followed such as the Sino-Japanese war (1894-1895) and in 1900, the Boxer Rebellion, which left thousands of Chinese dead.

In 1901, Wushu training was finally removed from the military and all the attention was placed to develop Civilian Wushu as a cultural, therapeutic and sportive activity, aside from the self-defense skills. Groups were established to encourage the practice of Wushu as a way to strengthen the body and also to promote national unity and moral values. In 1910, the Jingwu Athletic Association opened its doors in Shanghai, founded by Huo Yuanjia, who died within months of its actual establishment. The school gained recognition as its masters, originally from different Wushu styles, agreed to teach openly under the same roof, creating a more open environment for learning Wushu as opposed to the secretive training that had been common in the past. This fact is considered by some as the birth of the modern martial arts of China.

1.4. Modern Era (1912 - Present)

The Republic of China succeeded the Qing Dynasty in 1912, ending 2,000 years of imperial rule. Yet, multiple conflicts continued to take place as it evolved slowly through the Warlord Era (1916-1928) with the country divided by several military groups. In 1924, the Huangpu Military Academy was created in Guangdong in order to provide soldiers with military training. The academy witnessed the creation of a hand-to-hand combat method developed by various Wushu experts and Soviet advisors that could perfectly be a predecessor of the military Sanshou devised by the People's Liberation Army in the 1960s. Near the end of 1927, the Nationalist party earned control of China and started a decade of consolidation. Soon, terms like as "Guoyu" (National Language), "Guoyi" (National Medicine), "Guoju" (National Opera), "Guohua" (National Painting) and others were stipulated as official names as part of a program to popularize Nationalist values. Following this initiative, the term "Guoshu" (National Methods) - short for "Zhongguo Wushu" (Chinese Wushu) - became the official name for Chinese martial arts.

In 1928, the Central Guoshu Institute was established in Nanjing gathering many famous masters from several regions of the country to coordinate and disseminate martial arts. All major styles were organized into two major divisions: the Shaolin Faction for external styles like Shaolin, Chaquan, Tantui, Bajiquan, Piguaquan and others, lead by Wang Ziping; and the Wudang Faction for the internal styles like Taijiquan, Xingyiquan and Baguazhang, lead by Gao Zhendong. In addition, the Guoshu Physical Education Academy was also established with a mixed curriculum of Chinese martial arts and western sports such as boxing, fencing and wrestling, which acted energetically to modernize the martial skills and improve their teaching methods.

In 1928 and 1933, two national events were organized under the name of "Guoshu Guokao" (Guoshu National Examination) in Nanjing. Both meets included competitions of short and long weapon sparring, wrestling, male and female full-contact sparring and several other divisions. These hand-to-hand bouts were very fierce and according to some accounts, despite of the improvised protective equipment and very few rules that were implemented, there were far too many injuries and even deaths. Most of the top competitors became masters at the institute. Many provinces and cities opened their own Guoshu institutes and masters from the Central Guoshu Institute would teach in them. Most notorious for this were Gu Ruzhang, Wang Laisheng, Fu Zhensong, Wang Shaozhou and Li Xianwu known as the "Wu Hu Xia Jiang Nan" (Five tigers who went South), as they were assigned to move to the Guangdong-Guangxi Guoshu Institute to disseminate their northern arts. Later that year, Gu Ruzhang founded the Guangzhou Guoshu Association, and like him, many others followed suit.

Another important development during these years was the increasing number of martial arts manuals that appeared. Apart from important books, such as "Wu Shu Hui Zun" (The Root of Wushu) by Wang Laishen originally published in 1927, the Central Guoshu Institute launched a publishing department lead by Jiang Rongqiao were important manuals, magazines and newsletters were published. Guoshu Weekly, Guoshu Biweekly and others are examples of publications geared towards the community at large promoting the practice of martial arts openly. In 1933 and 1936, a delegation from the Central Guoshu Institute toured Hong Kong, Singapore, Malaysia, Indonesia and the Philippines. Later that year, as China organized and sent a full national team to the XI Olympic Games held in Berlin, a Guoshu demonstration team of eleven members was also included. The team performed several times in Berlin and Frankfurt bare-hand and weapon routines, sparring sets and Taijiquan group routines that were warmly welcomed by local observers and dignitaries. After the Olympics, the demonstrators went to Denmark, Sweden, Czechoslovakia, Hungary, Austria and Italy. The Central Guoshu Institute made indelible contributions to the development of Chinese martial arts, unfortunately, as the 2nd Sino-Japanese War erupted in 1937 and later merged into World War II, most of the accomplishments were dismantled completely.

Original poster from the 1953 National Ethnic Minorities Traditional Sports Games

In 1946, World War II ended but the Chinese Civil War resumed for another three years. During these wars, many outstanding Wushu experts fought in the army, others were forced to live in secrecy or to flee abroad; many were killed. In 1948, the Central Guoshu Institute was rebuilt in Tianjin, but as China continued to struggle, there was no funding available and the institute came to an end in 1948. However, not everything was lost, as some of its members later became well-known masters, professors or leaders of national organizations. For example, Wang Ziping was named vice-president of the Chinese Wushu Association in 1958. His student and member of the Chinese delegation that performed at the XI Olympic Games, Zhang Wenguang, is considered today as one of the creators of modern Wushu and was named vice-president of the Chinese Wushu Association in 1964. Another member of the same delegation, Zheng Huaixian, founded the Wushu department of the Chengdu Institute of Physical Education and was named president of the Chinese Wushu Association in 1980. And like them, many more helped to preserve the legacy of the Central Guoshu Institute.

Upon the proclamation of the People's Republic of China in 1949, the National Physical Culture and Sports Commission soon was established in order to reform sports in China and promote physical culture in general. In 1952, the first martial arts championship was held in Tianjin, following a similar format of the Guoshu National Examinations of the past including several routines, wrestling and full-contact sparring divisions. The term "Wushu" came back to replace the term "Guoshu" promoted by the Nationalists. In 1953, the National Ethnic Minorities Traditional Sports Games was held in Tianjin and more than 300 Wushu demonstrations were the center of it.

This dominance of Wushu among all traditional sports motivated the Sport Commission to engage in a project to rescue this important cultural legacy according to the policy: "to make the past serve the present, to let all flowers bloom and to weed through the old to bring forth the new". In 1954, the first China National Wushu team was setup at the Central Sports Institute, the predecessor of the Beijing University of Physical Education. During the following years, the first developments were accomplished fairly soon, heirs to the Wushu traditions were surveyed and several masters compiled the first modern forms. As part of this research and reform endeavor, Simplified and 88-Step Taijiquan, Simplified Taijijian, Three-Route Paoquan, Four-Route Chaquan, Six-Route Tantui and many other routines were prepared and published.

In 1958, a new legal organization was founded to manage the sport of Wushu on a national and international scale, the Chinese Wushu Association. And the same year, the first version of the Modern Wushu Competition Rules was published by the National Sports Commission. The new competition rules were used several times at special tournaments staged for farmers, workers and ethnic minorities, concluding with an important national competition in Beijing with the attendance of 27 provincial teams. Upon the establishment of the Chinese Wushu Association, the creators of modern Wushu like Zhang Wenguang, Cai Longyun, Chang Zhenfang, Zhou Yongfu and several other masters, worked upon the improvement of the sportive qualities and difficulties of Wushu combining the principles of sports science with the skills and theories of traditional Wushu. In 1959, the 1st China Sports Games were held in Guangzhou aimed at reviewing the achievements made in the past decade in terms of sports, and Wushu was included as one of the events.

Book co-author with Master Cai Longyun, one of the key originators of Contemporary Wushu.

The foundation of modern Wushu is Modern Changquan, a style created by combining the best elements of traditional northern styles such as Huaquan, Chaquan, Hongquan and others. Finally, the complete system was compiled and the new routines were classified according to their skill level into categories A, B and C, which included bare-hand routines as well as short, long and flexible weapon routines that were published successively. Later, the program was complemented with modern Nanquan, created upon elements from the five traditional southern family systems: Hong, Cai, Li, Liu and Mo; and a new Changquan routine was adapted for female athletes with more emphasis on flexibility and skillfulness. In 1962, the first set of Compulsory Competition Routines was published consisting of six events: Male Changquan, Female Changquan, Daoshu (Broadsword), Jianshu (Straightsword), Qiangshu (Spear) and Gunshu (Staff). In 1963, the Intermediate routines for each event were published as well to facilitate their learning at all levels.

During the following years, Wushu development continued as it became part of the curriculum of elementary, middle and high schools throughout China. In 1965, Wushu was present again in the 2nd China Sports Games held in Beijing. Unfortunately, the rapid growth of the sport stopped completely almost for one decade due to the Cultural Revolution (1966-1976). During most of

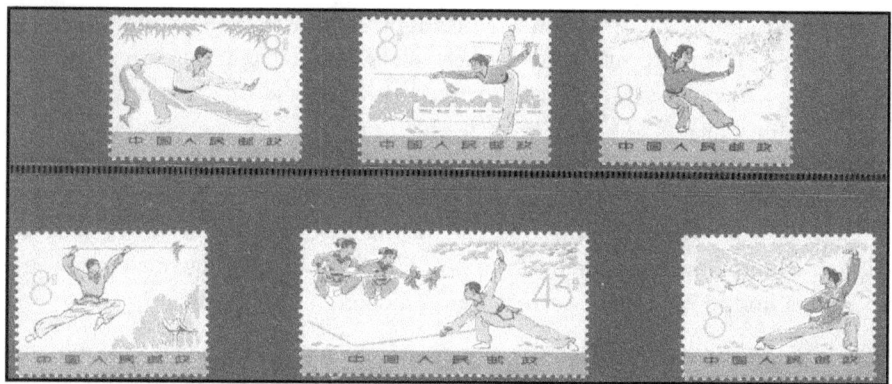

Commemorative Stamps issued to honor Contemporary Wushu in 1975.

these years, all forms of sports were suppressed in China. In 1969, the activist phase of the revolution was brought to an end and some sportive activities were encouraged as the state regained control. In 1971, the National Physical Culture and Sports Commission was restored and a year later the 1st Wushu competition at national level was celebrated in Shandong. In 1974, a national Wushu delegation visited the United States and Mexico, performing for President Nixon and Secretary of State Kissinger in the gardens of the White House. Undoubtedly, there was a noticeable resurgence of interest in Wushu. China's Sports Commission held the 3rd National Sports Games in 1975, the first one since the Cultural Revolution, and Wushu was included as an official event. In 1978, a research group was engaged in the efforts to develop the competition methods and rules for a sport version of Sanshou, the hand-to-hand combat discipline of Wushu that had been developing since early 1960s within the People's Liberation Army, grouping masters from all the country and defining a standard fighting style for close quarters.

In 1982, the National Physical Culture and Sports Commission and the Chinese Wushu Association held the 1st National Wushu Workshop in Beijing in order to review the achievements made, discuss new plans and future direction. The internationalization of the sport began under the slogan "Wushu originated in China but belongs to the world" and the first step was to send Wushu delegations around the world. In 1982 and 1983, as national and provincial teams toured the five continents, they met with enthusiastic audiences as well as critical acclaim. Also in 1982, the *1st China Wushu Friendship Demonstration Contest* was held in Nanjing. In 1983, an unprecedented three-year plan to carry on a state wide sampling of traditional Wushu styles was launched in order to rescue and record this important cultural legacy. More than 8000 professionals were selected and positioned strategically to perform their investigation tasks, hundreds of masters and their best students performed their routines and training methods, ancient weapons an old manuscripts were retrieved, etc. In total, 129 Wushu styles, 480 valuable Wushu articles and books, and 400 weapons were obtained.

In 1984, in response to the demands in this emerging field, Wushu was implemented in a number of schools as a Physical Education specialty, both at Bachelor's and Master's Degree levels. Also that year, the Chinese Wushu Association organized an international Wushu symposium in Wuhan to discuss about the possibilities of establishing an international Wushu organization. In 1985, a five-level Wushu athlete rank system was implemented, comprised of "Wu Ying" (Martial Hero) level, "Wu Shi" (Martial Scholar) level one, two and three; and "Wu Tong" (Martial Child) level for junior athletes. The competition rules and general competition format were revised; the events were grouped into four categories: Empty Hand Routines, Weapon Routines,

Sparring Sets and Group Routines. Athletes were requested to perform compulsory and optional routines and the all-around championship titles were calculated upon five events.

In 1985, three main milestones were achieved, in August the 1st International Wushu Invitational Tournament was held in Xi'an with participation of 98 athletes from 12 countries. During the event, the Preparatory Committee for the International Wushu Federation was established by representatives of China, England, Italy, Japan and Singapore. And in November, the European Wushu Federation was founded as the first continental Wushu Federation. In 1986, the National Physical Culture and Sports Commission and the Chinese Wushu Association organized a national conference to present the results from the national survey on traditional Wushu in Beijing. More than 200 people from 28 provinces and 13 physical education universities were in attendance. That same year, the Chinese Wushu Research Institute was founded to pursue and coordinate further investigations on Wushu.

Also in 1986, the 2nd International Wushu Invitational Tournament was held in Tianjin with participation of 145 athletes from 20 countries. The Wushu Federation of South America was founded that same year. In 1987, the Chinese Wushu Association successfully organized the 1st International Coaches Seminar in Shenzhen with 47 participants of 13 countries. That same year, the 6th National Sport Games in Guangdong had Wushu as an official medal sport with 16 events and the Asian Wushu Federation was established.

In 1988, Sanshou was officially added to the national Wushu competition format of China. Later that year, the 3rd International Wushu Invitational Tournament was held in two cities, the Taolu portion of the competition took place in Hangzhou with participation of 202 athletes from 31 countries; the Sanshou portion was held in Shenzhen with participation of 60 athletes from 15 countries. In 1989, the Chinese Wushu Association was busy developing a new set of rules to be used at international level. The scope of the project included the compilation of the 1st Set of International Compulsory Routines for seven events: Changquan, Nanquan, Taijiquan, Daoshu, Jianshu, Qiangshu and Gunshu. These routines, excluding Taijiquan, were simplified versions of the competition routines of the Chinese athletes Yuan Wenqing, Zhao Changjun, Chen Lihong and Peng Ying; all very famous national champions. Also in 1989, Sanshou made its debut as an official event of the National Wushu Championships with participation of 146 athletes from 26 teams, and the African Wushu Federation was founded.

In 1990, the International Wushu Federation was finally established as the world governing body of the sport of Wushu and the Olympic Council of Asia granted Wushu as an official medal sport at the Asian Sports Games, a great accomplishment towards the internationalization of the sport. Later that year, 96 Wushu athletes from 11 countries participated at the 11th Asian Sports Games in Beijing and tested the new international rules for the first time. In 1991, according to the federation plan of organizing world competitions every two years, the 1st World Wushu Championships were held in Beijing in 1991, the Taolu event was very successful with participation of more than 500 athletes from 40 countries, and although the International Compulsory Routines were not enforced, a good number of athletes performed them in competition. In 1992, the National Physical Culture and Sports Commission and the Chinese Wushu Association held the 2nd National Wushu Workshop in Sichuan where the previous 10 years of work were summarized and new strategic targets were proposed and decided at national and international level.

In 1993, the 7th National Sport Games were held in Chengdu and the 2nd World Wushu

Championships were held in Kuala Lumpur and Sanshou was included for the first time as an official medal sport in such events. In 1994, International Wushu Federation was recognized by the General Assembly of International Sports Federations, an organism of the International Olympic Committee that coordinates all Olympic sports. In 1995, the Pan American Wushu Federation was founded and later the 3rd World Wushu Championships were held in Baltimore and the results were very encouraging as nearly 800 athletes from 68 countries participated. In 1996, the first Doctoral Degree in Wushu was approved in China, initiated by the Shanghai Institute of Physical Education. Also in 1996, the third National Wushu Workshop convened in Tianjin and new changes were formulated to the national competition format. The Chinese Wushu Association recognized that, as Wushu athletes hone their skills and continue to perform at a very high level, judges were in the need of better methods to determine the winning scores. Consequently, competitors were forced to include within their optional routines a choice of two High Difficulty Movements consisting of a compulsory combination of techniques, mostly jumps and balances, published by the association per event and gender. This new measure affected not only the judging criteria, but also the training methods of elite athletes.

In 1997, China celebrated the 8th National Sports Games in Shanghai, and Wushu was the only non-Olympic sport with 28 divisions grouped into 15 medal events. Following Shanghai's games, the 4th World Wushu Championships were held in Rome, where international athletes were able to demonstrate remarkable progress in terms of their basic skills. Later that year, the Chinese Wushu Association introduced to the world a newly developed ranking system consisting of nine levels, usually referred by their Chinese name or "Duan". The new promotion system adopted three animals: Eagle, Tiger and Dragon; and three colors: Blue, Silver and Golden; to indicate a specific level of Wushu respectively. The lowest rank that is awarded is a 1st Duan or Blue Eagle, and the highest rank is 9th Duan or Golden Dragon, reserved for those who have contributed greatly to the development and preservation of the sport of Wushu.

In 1999, International Olympic Committee granted provisional recognition to the International Wushu Federation. Later in 1999, the 5th World Wushu Championships were held in Hong Kong where three new events were added to the official competition program: Nandao, Nangun and Taijijian; and encouraging results were achieved as the technical level of the international competitors continued to be on the rise. In 2000, new reforms for the sport of Wushu were set in place at the Fourth National Wushu workshop was held in Anhui. For instance, the Chinese Wushu Association implemented a new set of High Difficulty Movements to be used at the national Taolu competitions and agreed upon the use of the term "Sanda" (Free Fighting) to refer to Sanshou within the country, while the name Sanshou continued to be used internationally. It was also determined, based on the technical progress achieved by the international competitors, that the International Wushu Federation will assemble a technical committee to compile the 2nd Set of International Compulsory Routines on five of the original seven competition events: Changquan, Daoshu, Gunshu, Jianshu and Qiangshu. But perhaps, the major milestone accomplished by the Chinese Wushu Association that year was to launch for the first time a professional tournament called King of Sanda, an ambitious effort to promote Sanda into a nationwide sport including weekly TV broadcasts and a final match that combined all weight classes.

In 2001, following Beijing's successful bid to host the 2008 Olympic Games and confident that the sport would finally be included in the official Olympic program, the International Wushu

Federation stepped into a new era of developments to meet the Olympic strict standards. In the light of the new requirements, a radically new system of judging was implemented awarding points for technical elements based on a prior analysis of each element's difficulty degree - a jumping inside kick with a rotation of 720 degrees gets more base points than a standard a jumping inside kick - as well as the transition or connecting moves, the quality of movements and the overall performance of the competitor. The panel of judges is now composed of one head judge and nine judges divided into groups A, B and C. Responsible for the quality of movement are the judges of group A, the ones of group B for the overall performance, and the ones of group C for the difficulty degree. Aside from the new rules, it was necessary to determine the appropriate program to best represent Wushu in the Olympics, and the commission selected the following eight medal events: Changquan, Nanquan, Daoshu and Gunshu for male; and Changquan, Taijiquan, Jianshu and Qiangshu for female. Sanshou was not included primarily because of the fact that the Olympic program already has several other combat disciplines.

In March of the same year, the 1st World Taijiquan Conference was held in Hainan. This new type of venture by the International Wushu Federation proved to be very successful, gathering Taiji enthusiasts from around the world. The meet included a full schedule of classes on the standard routines of 1st, 2nd and 3rd Duan of Taijiquan; routines of the traditional styles Yang, Chen, Sun, Wu and Wu (Hao); as well as an official competition of Taijiquan and Taijijian divided into four groups based on age. Later in November, the 6th World Wushu Championships were held in Yerevan and the 2nd Set of International Compulsory Routines were implemented for the first time. At Yerevan, old and new International Compulsory Routines were allowed in separate divisions. In November, the 9th China Sports Games were held in Guangzhou and the Chinese government invited 46 International Olympic Committee officials, including President Jacques Rogge, to attend. A special Wushu demonstration by top Chinese athletes was presented to them as an introduction to the sport in a clear effort to strengthen the relations between both organisms. In December 10, the International Wushu Federation signed the Drug Testing Service Agreement with the World Anti-Doping Agency. Therefore, Wushu athletes are requested to comply with the anti-doping program established by the International Olympic Committee. And only ten days later, the International Wushu Federation officially submitted the Olympic proposal package to the International Olympic Committee, including an introductory video, several photo booklets, the list of medal events, the general rules for competition, the criteria for athlete selection, a proposed competition schedule and other basic information.

In 2002, the International Olympic Committee officially recognized the International Wushu Federation and accepted its application to be listed as a medal event in February alongside other sports. Later in August, 18 of those applications were formally rejected and Wushu was confirmed for further study. That same year, the International Wushu Federation organized the 1st Sanshou World Cup in Shanghai gathering the top Sanshou athletes from the last World and Continental Championships and offering money prizes for the first places. In 2003, the 7th World Wushu Championships were held in Macau. Female Sanshou and Sparring Sets were added for the first time at this event. Also, it was noted that the international athletes were able to perform the 2nd Set of International Compulsory Routines with great skill and coordination, demonstrating their overall improvement in training methods and in Wushu in general. On November of that same year, the first International Wushu and Olympic Culture conference was held in Macao, in order to discuss the potential cultural implications and difficulties of integrating Wushu to the Olympic

Movement.

In 2004, the 1st World Traditional Wushu Festival was held in Henan. which topped all previous Wushu events in terms of scale and number of participants. It included ceremonies, demonstrations, competitions, seminars and Wushu Duan examinations with participation of nearly 1300 athletes from 62 countries. Also in 2004, the 2nd World Taijiquan Conference and the 2nd Sanshou World Cup were held in Hainan and Guangzhou respectively. The successful organization of events like the King of Sanda, the World Taijiquan Conference, the Sanshou World Cup or the Traditional Wushu Festival clearly represent the efforts by the Chinese Wushu Association and the International Wushu Federation diversifying into different initiatives and different targets to further accelerate the popularization of Wushu in the world.

In, 2005, 10th China Sports Games were held in Jiangsu, and Wushu continued to be the only non-Olympic sport with a total of 18 medal events, 12 for Taolu and 6 for Sanshou. The Chinese Wushu Association, as part of their unceasing effort of innovation introduced several new elements to the Taolu competition. For example, the competition carpet has been enhanced to a tapered padded floor mainly to reduce the impact from the high difficulty jumps and other acrobatic moves. Also the size of the competition area has increased to 15m x 8m of usable space. On the other hand, competitors are allowed to add instrumental music to their bare-hand routines and wear elaborate costumes instead of mandatory solid color silk uniforms specified in the old rules. Later that year, the new competition rules were partially implemented at the 8th World Wushu Championships held in Hanoi. At this event, the international competitors exceeded all expectations, demonstrating their much improved preparation and athletic level.

Unfortunately, despite all the efforts, shortly after the 8th World Championships, the International Olympic Committee announced that Wushu was not going be part of the official sports of the 2008 Beijing Olympic Games a few days after the World Championships of Hanoi. "There will be a Wushu competition during the Olympic Games. It's not going to be one of the official 28 sports but we will organize with BOCOG (the Beijing Organizing Committee for the Games of the XXIX Olympiad) a Wushu competition" said Jacques Rogge, president of the International Olympic Committee. This decision was received with considerable disappointment by most contemporary Wushu practitioners, coaches and organizers, although not all was lost, since being able to organize an international Wushu tournament in Beijing parallel to the Olympic Games remains a major milestone and a landmark in the development of the sport. And the International Wushu Federation did not cease on their efforts of promotion and continued to further make changes and organize different types of events such as the 2nd World Traditional Wushu Festival in Henan, the 3rd Sanshou World Cup in Xi'an and the 1st World Junior Wushu Championships organized in Kuala Lumpur, during the year 2006.

Currently, all the eyes of the international Wushu community, over one hundred and eleven members from all five continents, are mainly focused on the 9th World Wushu Championships that will be held in Beijing in November of 2007. This competition will determine the world's top 120 athletes from 25 countries, including Sanshou and Taolu, which will be earning a spot at the 2008 Olympic Beijing Wushu Tournament. Looking into the future, this competition will be a fantastic opportunity to showcase Wushu to the world; it will be another defining moment on the history of Wushu - history in the making!

Chapter 2

Wushu Basic Skills

The basic skills of Wushu, generally referred as basics (Ji Ben Gong), are the essential fundamentals - the building blocks - for becoming an accomplished Wushu practitioner. They encompass a wide array of techniques, exercises and drills divided in eight areas of instruction. They are: stretching and flexibility exercises, hand forms and hand techniques, stances and footwork, leg techniques, basic combinations, balance techniques, jumping techniques and tumbling techniques. In order to gain proficiency in Wushu the objective should always be to build up a strong foundation first and later work upon integrating and refining all the independent parts as a whole.

The process of learning basic skills is a long-term commitment. Beginners should practice the basic skills of Wushu at a comfortable level, with an emphasis on understanding the requirements of each movement while building up athletic attributes such as strength, flexibility, balance, agility and coordination. It is imperative to learn to execute all techniques in a correct and clean manner prior to thinking about adding speed or power. Correct technique and quality repetition is the key to learning skills, not to say that hard training is not necessary, but sometimes the wrong kind of training can do more damage than good.

Bear in mind that "basic" skills are not necessarily "easy" skills. For instance, let's take one of the most popular Wushu techniques - the jumping inside slap kick. This movement consists of a vertical jump, a spin of the waist, an inside slap kick performed in midair and an accurate jump reception. For each part, there are numerous skills involved, for example explosive force and good spring to acquire the ideal jump height; strong waist, stomach and back muscles to facilitate the spinning motion; good flexibility and leg power to kick close to the body and make a loud slap; and many more.

Ironically, a proper jumping inside slap kick can be completed in a split of a second by an experienced practitioner, but gaining such proficiency usually takes several years of continuous practice. Again, the teaching/learning process of the basic skills of Wushu is a long one, and unfortunately, there are no shortcuts. Following a systematic and integrative training program, such as the one described on this book, is the only way to guarantee a successful and safe Wushu career.

2.1. Stretching and Flexibility Training

Stretching and flexibility exercises of Wushu refer to a series of stretches and active mobility exercises that aim to provide the practitioner with flexibility, pliability and range of motion specific to the requirements of Wushu. There are different types of movements that require different types of flexibility. For instance, holding a forward balance for a few seconds or assuming a very low drop stance calls for good static flexibility, while performing a high speed kick at head level involves dynamic flexibility. On this section we have included some the most common stretching and flexibility exercises that will help you improve in both areas. As you progress through them, there are many variations that can be added.

Practice your Wushu stretches diligently and regularly, ideally twice a day, every day. Start every stretching session with a generic warm-up followed by the step-by-step guides provided on this chapter. Beginner and intermediate practitioners must invest time and energy to improve their flexibility, while advanced practitioners need to work hard to maintain it. Flexibility is affected by a number of factors, learn to measure your progress and always refrain from excessive exertion, stretching should never be painful, even though, those gaining new ranges of motion are expected to feel mild soreness in their muscles. Slow static stretching and gentle massaging can help to reduce muscle soreness after practice. Advanced practitioners may adapt to a routine that best suits them and work harder on those specific areas that could still be lacking.

Once again, keep in mind the importance of using stretching methods that meet the specific requirements of Wushu. A typical runner hamstring stretch may not suffice for a beginner that is looking to achieve the desired mobility to perform a proper front stretch kick. Moreover, if that is how you stretch, that is how you will kick! Wushu specific stretching methods traditionally include passive static stretching (i.e. doing the splits), active static stretching (i.e. holding stances, leg balances), dynamic stretching (i.e. performing leg swings, stretch kicks) and ballistic stretching (i.e. performing gentle bounces over a stretch within its range of motion). Furthermore, there are additional methods, not covered on this volume for space reasons, such as PNF and other partner-assisted stretches, which are highly recommended for improving flexibility and strength.

There is some controversy as to whether ballistic stretching methods are recommended. Commonly, ballistic stretching is used by Wushu athletes to simulate specific dynamic actions of the physical activity they are training for. Take a front stretch kick, you may notice that as the kick goes up towards your forehead and reaches its maximum straight leg hip flexion, there is a wiping motion that exerts pressure on the knee joint and on certain muscles of the leg and lower back, right before the leg starts to come down. This type of muscle activity, especially the one requiring a burst of speed, is a good example of what elite athletes need to be prepared for. Therefore, Wushu incorporates all the different categories of stretching methods mentioned on this chapter, which should always be performed strictly under qualified supervision, controlled conditions and taking all the necessary precautions.

Palm Stretch (Ya Zhang)

Grasp one of your hands in front of your chest and apply pressure over the palm/fingers side bending the wrist back (Fig. 2.1). For a further stretch, straighten the arm of the wrist that is being stretched in front of you while the pressure is being applied (Fig. 2.2). Alternatively, you can twist your wrist 180 degrees so your fingers point to the floor (Fig. 2.3). Hold each stretch at least 20 seconds.

Fig. 2.1

Fig. 2.2

Fig. 2.3

Special Tips: Relax the arm, keep the elbow straight and concentrate the stretching on the wrist. Additionally, you may bring both hands in front of your chest, interlace fingers and perform circular movements to relax the wrists after the performing these stretches.

Shoulder Stretch (Ya Jian)

Stand with your feet shoulder width apart facing an object of at least waist height. Place both palms on it and lean forward. Bend by the waist keeping the arms and legs straight. Sink down your back and shoulders as low as possible (Fig. 2.4).

Fig. 2.4

A variation of this exercise is to stand with your feet shoulder width apart facing away from an object of at least waist height. Place both palms on it and bend both legs to a full squat keeping the arms straight (Fig. 2.5).

Special Tips: Relax the arms, keep the elbows straight and concentrate the stretching on the shoulders. Keep the distance between the hands as close as possible. Hold each stretch at least 20 seconds.

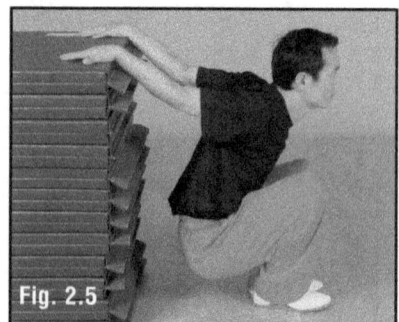
Fig. 2.5

Arm Rotations (Bi Rao Huan)

Assume a left bow stance and place your left hand on your waist. Extend your right arm and make circles by rotating at the shoulder. Keep your elbow straight (Fig. 2.6 to Fig. 2.9). Arm rotations can be done forward or backward. Repeat the exercise on the opposite side.

Fig. 2.6

Fig. 2.7

Fig. 2.8

Fig. 2.9

Mastering Wushu

A variation of this exercise is to stand with feet shoulder width apart, extending both arms and making circles by rotating at the shoulder. Keep your elbows straight. Arm rotations can be done simultaneously with both arms forward, simultaneously with both arms backward or alternately with on arm forward and the other backward (Fig. 2.10 to Fig. 2.13).

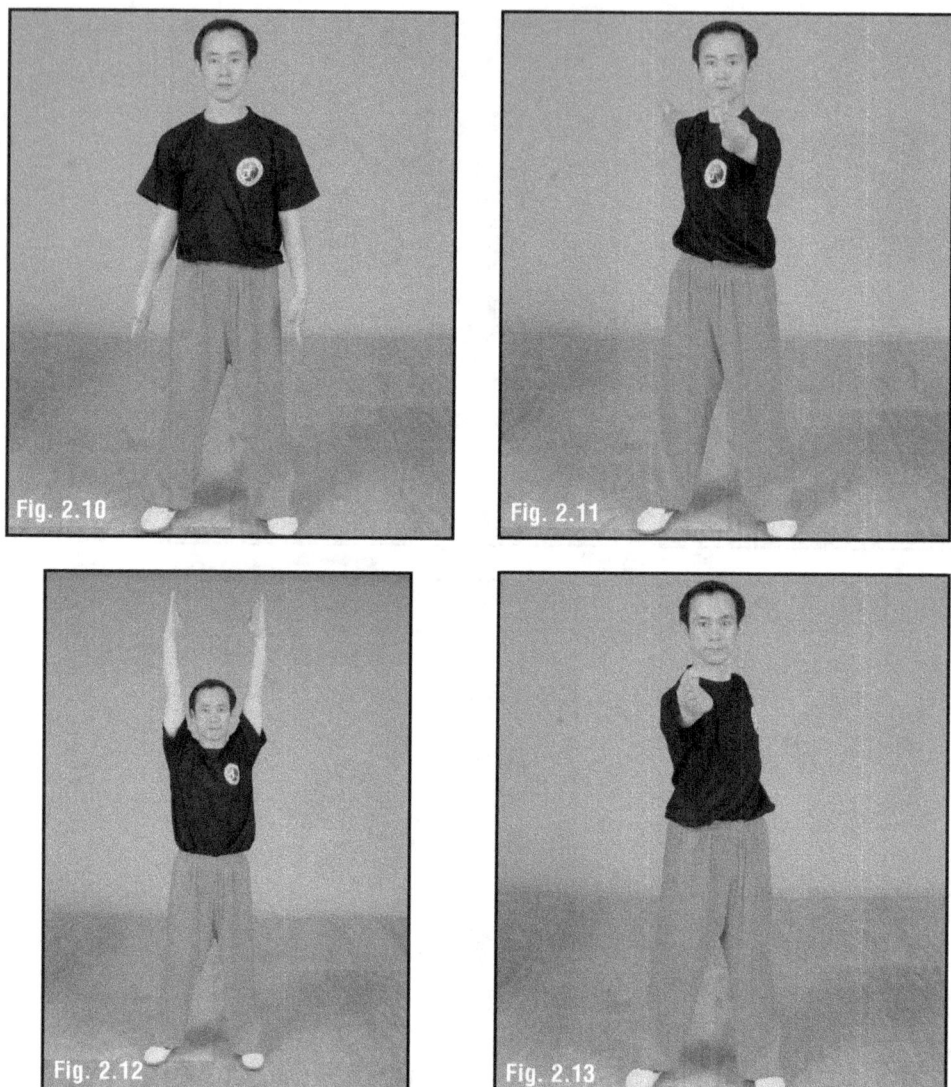

Special Tips: Relax the arms, keep fingers pointed and shoulder and back relaxed. Look to the front. Keep arms always in a vertical plane. Increase the speed and the intensity.

Knee Bends and Rotations (Xi Bu Yun Dong)

Stand with your feet together. Place your hands on your knees for stability. Start with your legs straight and press against your knees (Fig. 2.14), then release the tension and bend them into a half squat (Fig. 2.15). Perform circular movements with both knees together in both directions (Fig. 2.16 to Fig. 2.17).

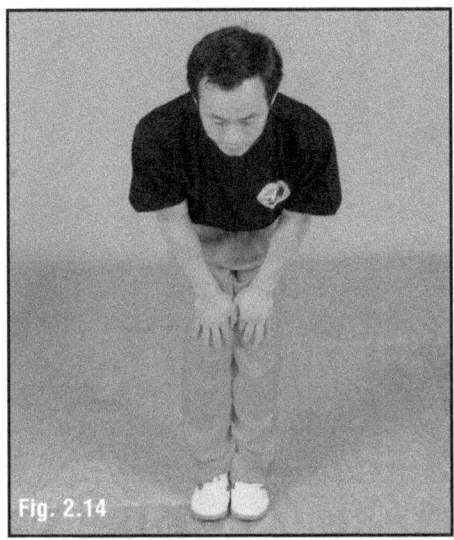
Fig. 2.14

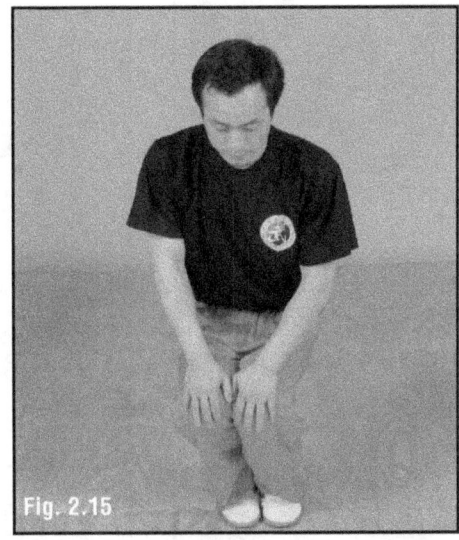
Fig. 2.15

Fig. 2.16

Fig. 2.17

A variation of this exercise is to perform opening and closing motions with your legs, again pressing and releasing tension with your hands on your knees (Fig. 2.18 to Fig. 2.21).

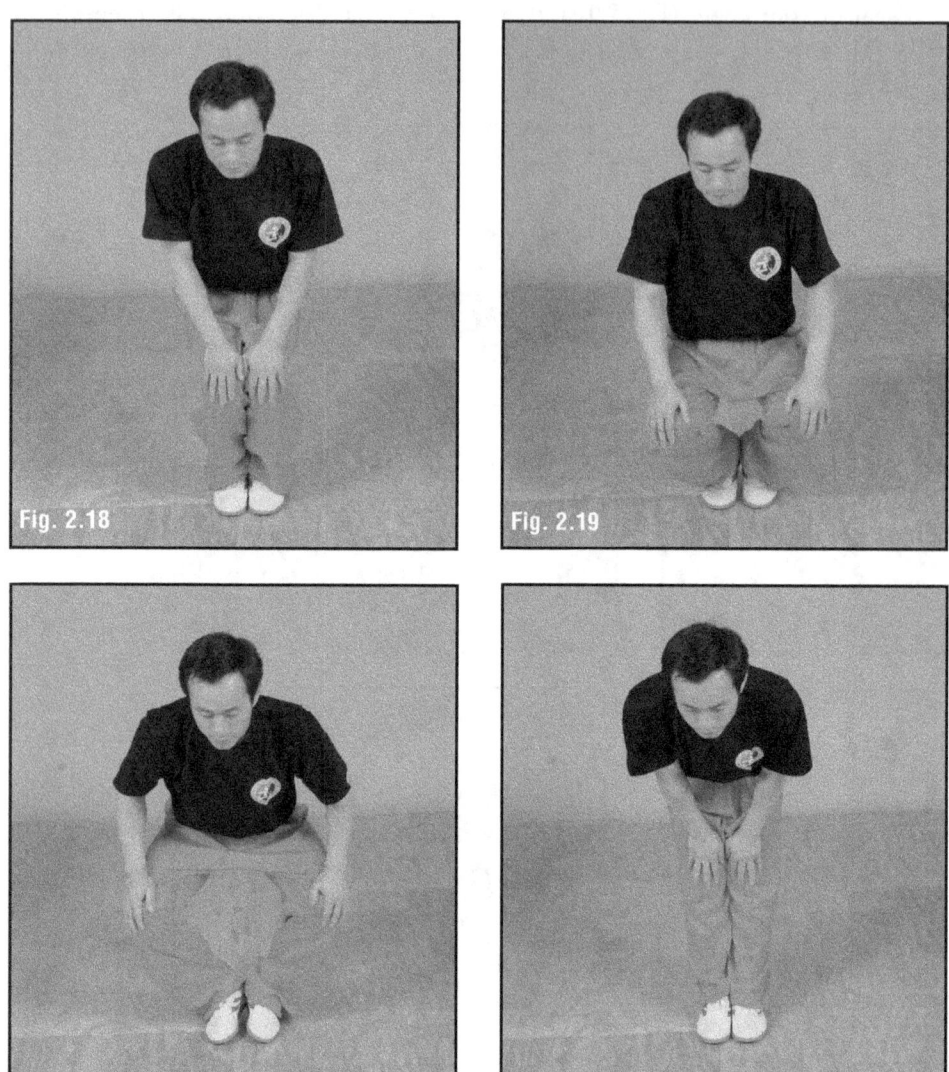

Special Tips: Keep both feet flat on the ground as much as possible and support your weight through the center of your body. You should also go down to full squat as part of the same exercise.

Leaning Ankle Stretch (Ya Huai)

Stand facing a wall or another similar object and place both hands on it. Assume a right bow stance (Fig. 2.22). Press the body forward by leaning towards the wall, keeping the body and left knee straight and the left foot flat on the ground (Fig. 2.23). For a further stretch, bend the left knee as forward as possible without allowing the left heel to come off the floor. Repeat the exercise on the opposite side.

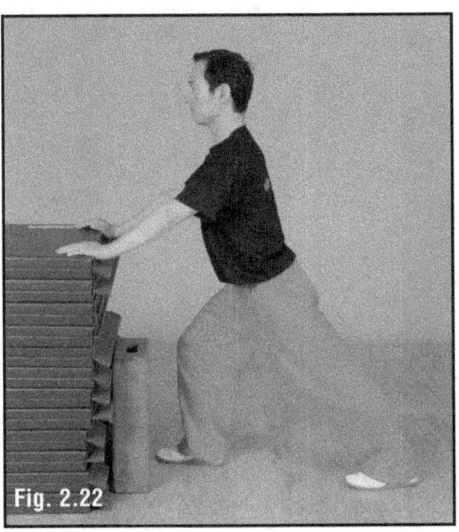
Fig. 2.22

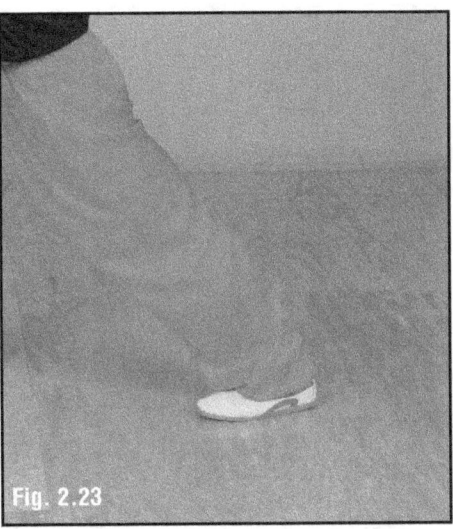
Fig. 2.23

A variation of this exercise is to place the toes of one of your feet against the wall with the heel resting on the floor (Fig. 2.24). Press your body forward by leaning towards the wall (Fig. 2.25). Repeat the exercise on the opposite side.

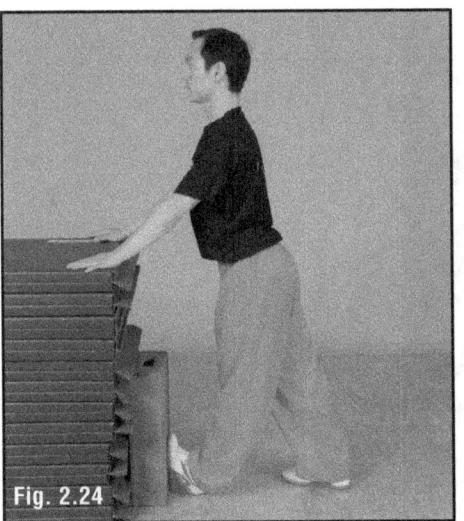
Fig. 2.24

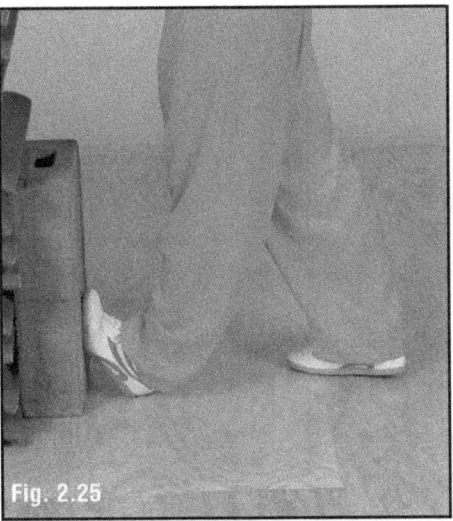
Fig. 2.25

Special Tips: Always keep the toes of the stretching leg pointing forward and concentrate the stretch on the Achilles tendon area. Hold each stretch at least 20 seconds.

Kneeling Instep Stretch (Gui Ya)

Kneel down on the floor with your back straight (Fig. 2.26). Lean back and support your body with your hands flat on the floor (Fig. 2.27). Shift your weight backwards over to your arms, lift both knees and try to keep both feet on the ground supported on the insteps first and ultimately on the tip of your toes (Fig. 2.28).

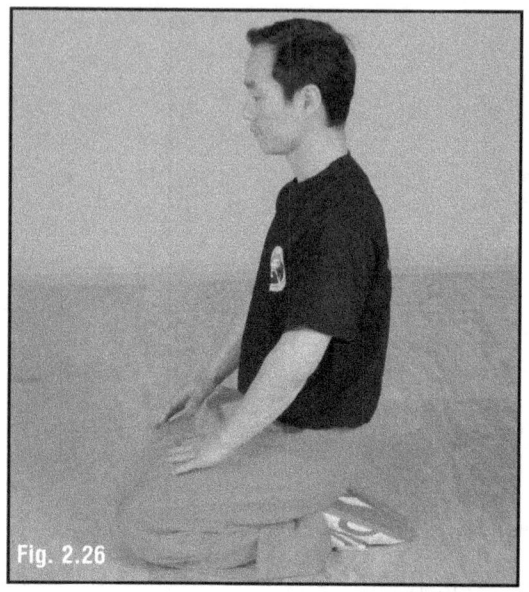

Fig. 2.26

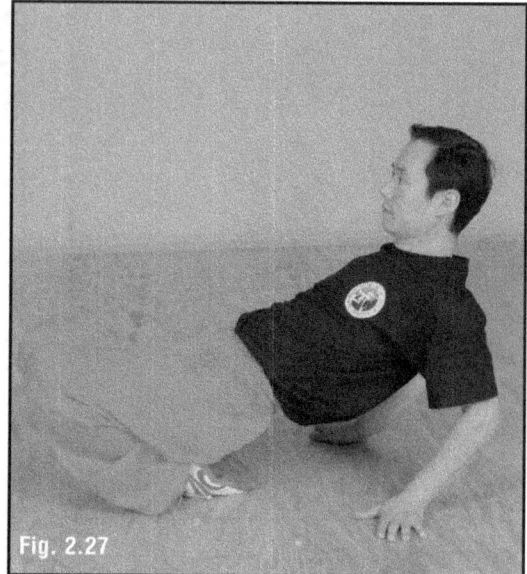

Fig. 2.27

Fig. 2.28

Special Tips: Always keep the toes of the stretching leg pointing forward and concentrate the stretch on the instep area. Hold the stretch at least 20 seconds.

Drop Stance Stretch (Pu Ya)

Assume a left drop stance; grab your left foot with your left hand and your right foot with your right hand (Fig. 2.29), switch from right drop stance to left drop stance as you stretch your legs and hips (Fig. 2.30). Repeat the exercise on the opposite side.

Fig. 2.29

Fig. 2.30

A variation of this exercise is to assume a left drop stance and grab your left foot with both hands while you try to keep your stance as low as possible (Fig. 2.31). Repeat the exercise on the opposite side (Fig. 2.32).

Fig. 2.31

Fig. 2.32

Special Tips: Keep both feet flat on the ground and point your toes forward. Keep your body as low as possible throughout the whole movement. Hold each stretch at least 20 seconds.

Wheeling Arms Slap Floor in Drop Stance (Wu Long Pan Da)

Assume a left bow stance with your right arm stretched out (Fig. 2.33). Swing your right arm upwards in an arc while you turn your body and waist to the right and stretch out the left arm (Fig. 2.34 to Fig. 2.36). Continue to rotate both arms; your right arm downward and upwards on the right side of your body and the left arm goes upwards and downwards on the left side of your body (Fig. 2.37 to Fig. 2.39). Complete the movement by assuming a right drop stance and slapping the floor with your right palm in front of the right foot. Stretch the left arm to the left above head level (Fig. 2.40). Repeat the exercise in the opposite direction.

Fig. 2.33

Fig. 2.34

Fig. 2.35

Fig. 2.36

Fig. 2.37

Fig. 2.38

Fig. 2.39

Fig. 2.40

Special Tips: All movements should be performed in one single motion. Use the waist to guide the arms. Keep arms always straight and slap the floor at the same time you complete the drop stance.

Hip Rotations (Shuan Yao)

Assume a right hooked leg half squat balance and thrust your right arm forward. Look to the right (Fig. 2.41). Step left with your left leg to assume a right bow stance (Fig. 2.42). Swing your right arm over your left arm in a circular motion around the center of your body. Bend your knees slightly and shift the weight of the body to the center (Fig. 2.43 to Fig. 2.44). Continue to swing your arms and follow with your trunk leftward, backward, rightward and forward (Fig. 2.45 to Fig. 2.51). Assume a left bow stance and finish the movement (Fig. 2.52). Repeat the exercise in the opposite direction.

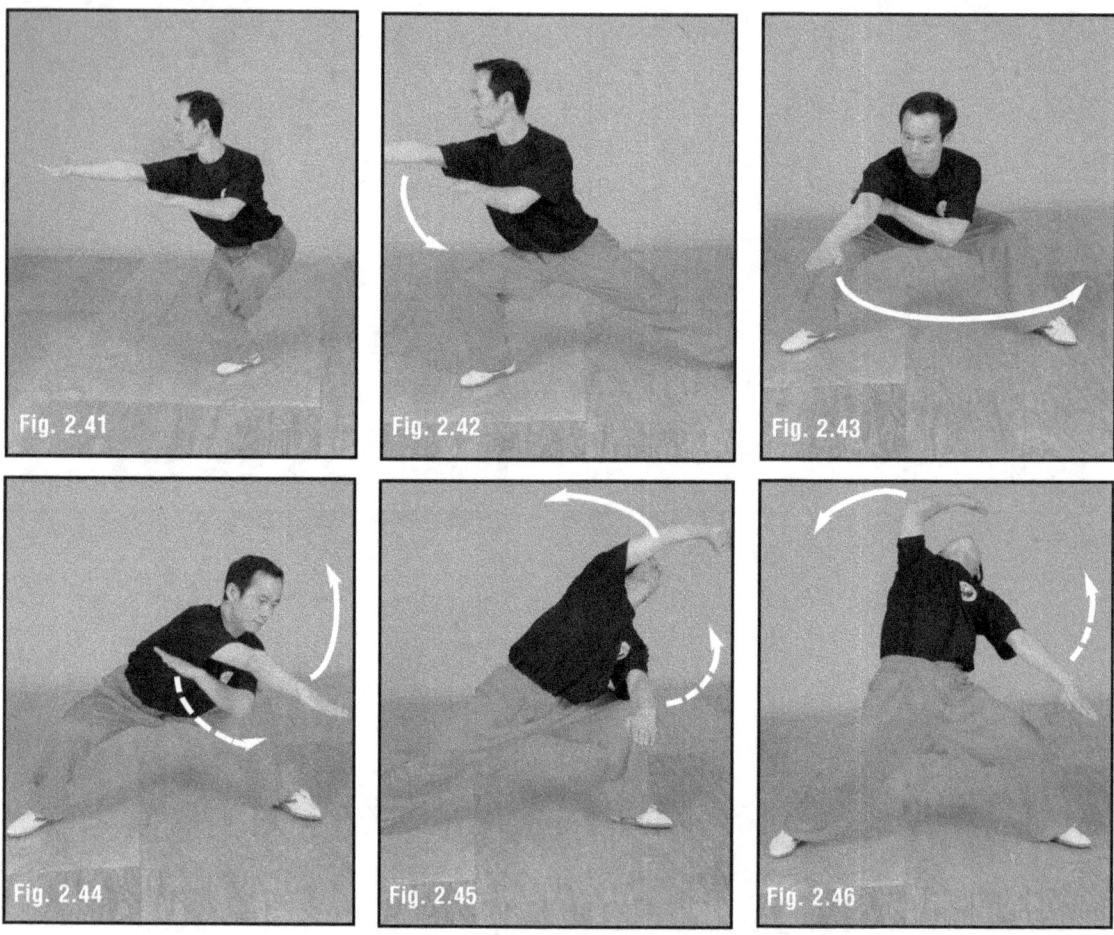

Chapter 2

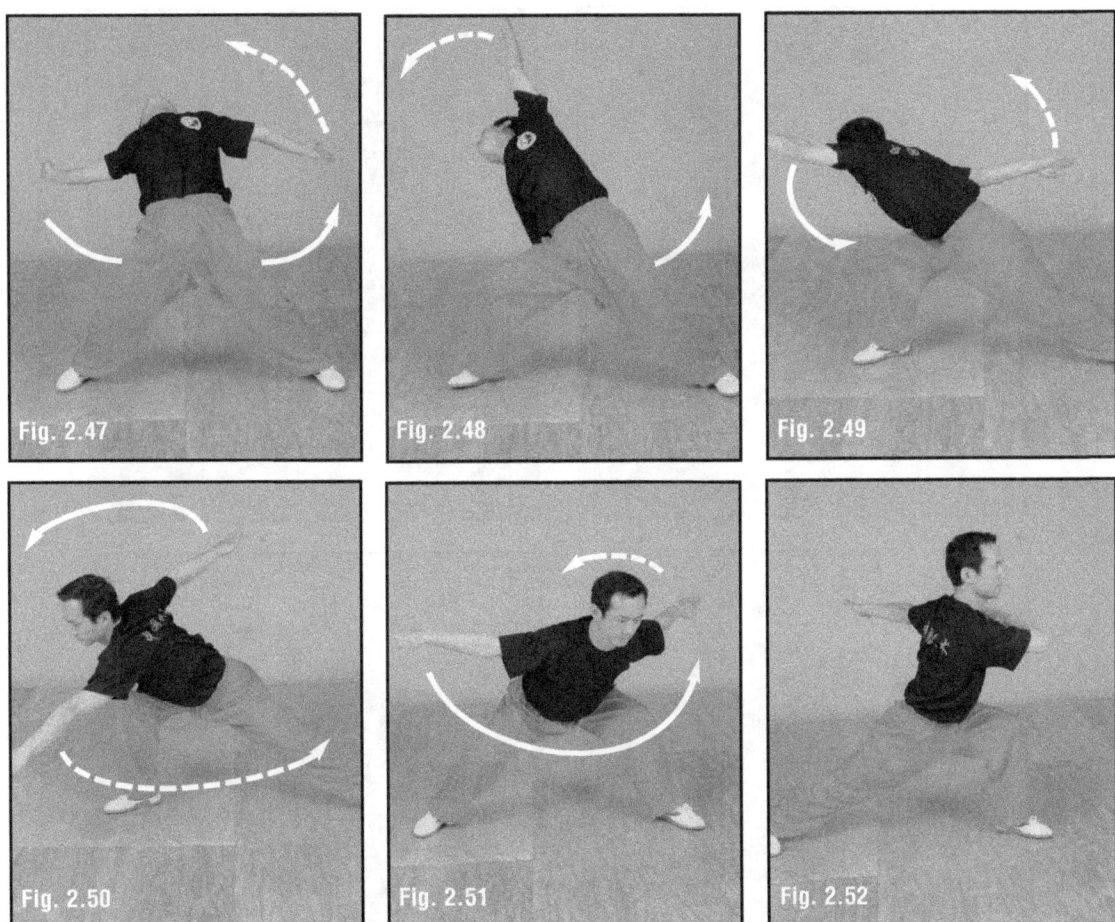

Fig. 2.47　　　　Fig. 2.48　　　　Fig. 2.49
Fig. 2.50　　　　Fig. 2.51　　　　Fig. 2.52

Special Tips: All movements should be performed in one single motion. Bend the knees and lower your center of gravity as you reach with your arms as far as possible to the left, back, right and front.

Front Leg Stretch (Zheng Ya Tui)

Stand with feet together facing an object of at least waist height. Raise one leg and place the heel on the object, toes upward, ankle flexed. Press both hands on the knee (Fig. 2.53) as you gently lean your body forward (Fig. 2.54) and return to the upright position. Repeat the exercise 8 times with each leg. Then hold the stretch on each side for at least 20 seconds. As you make progress, you may grab the raised foot with both hands and pull your foot back with both arms as you lean forward (Fig. 2.55). You should aim to touch your toes to your forehead, then your nose, mouth and chin (Fig. 2.56).

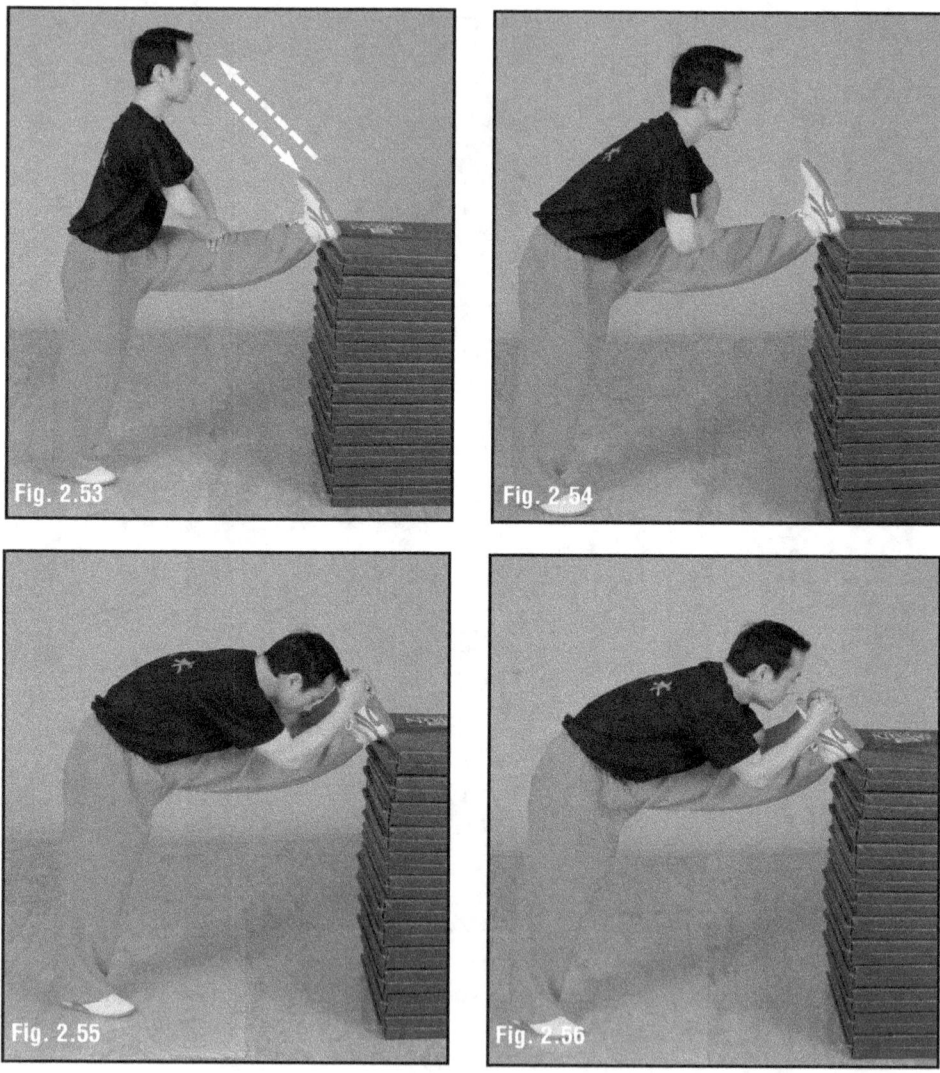

Special Tips: Keep the chest out, the hips squared and the buttocks in. Keep both legs straight. Bend the body at the waist and keep your upper body straight. Bend both elbows when pulling the foot back. Make sure to never stress the knee joint out of its range of motion.

Side Leg Stretch (Ce Ya Tui)

Stand with feet together side on to an object of at least waist height. Raise the leg closer to the object and place the heel on top, toes upward, ankle flexed. Left arm is bent by the elbow and placed in front of the right side of the chest. Right arm is raised straight up (Fig. 2.57). Gently lean your body to the side (Fig. 2.58), touch the toes of the raised foot with the hand of the extended arm (Fig. 2.59) and return to the upright position. Repeat the exercise 8 times with each leg. Then hold the stretch on each side for at least 20 seconds. As you make progress, you grab the raised foot and bring your body as close to the leg as possible while you pull with your arm. You should aim to touch your toes to your head (Fig. 2.60).

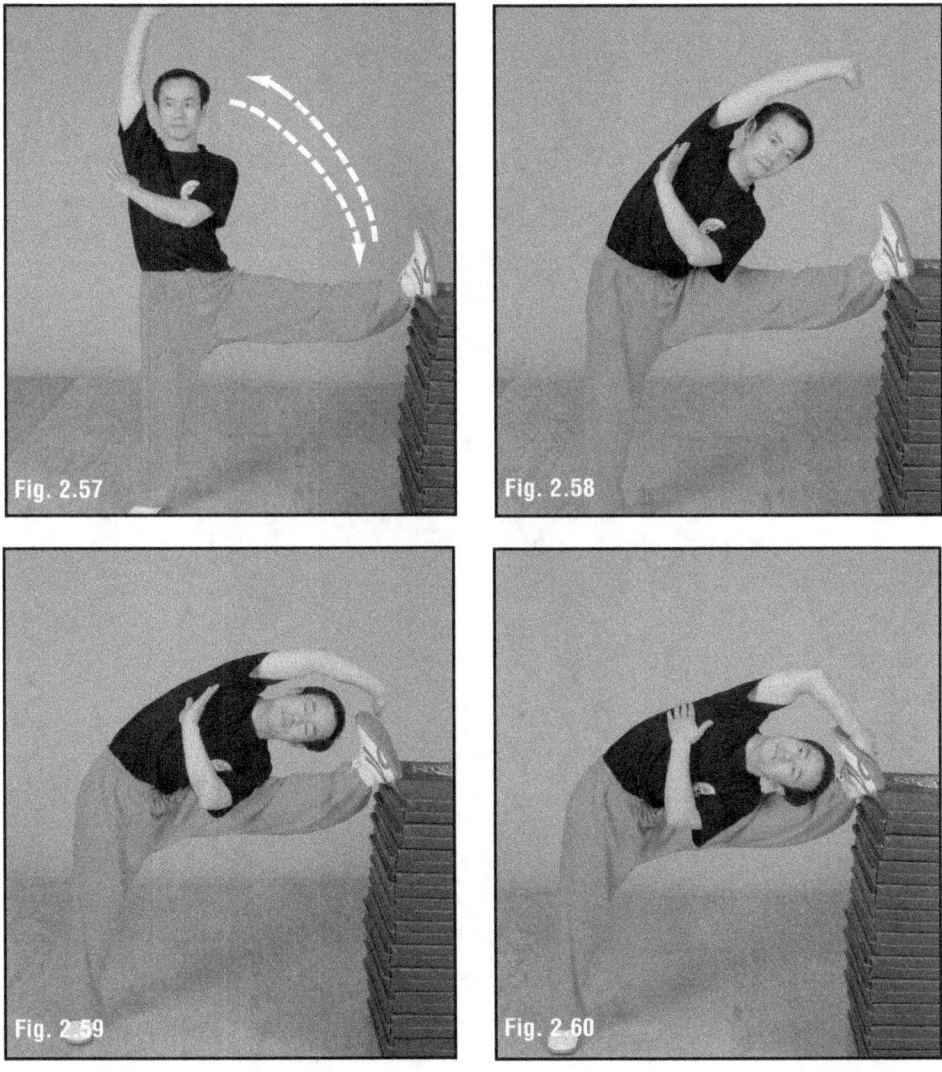

Special Tips: Special Tips: Keep the chest out and the buttocks in. Keep both legs straight. Bend the body at the waist and keep your upper body straight. You may grab the raised foot with both hands and touch your toes with your ear. Make sure to never stress the knee joint out of its range of motion.

Back Leg Stretch (Hou Ya Tui)

Stand with feet together facing away of an object of at least waist height. Lift and extend one leg to the rear and place the instep on the object. Keep both arms are holding your waist (Fig. 2.61). Bend the body backwards arching your neck and back as much as possible (Fig. 2.62). Repeat the exercise 8 times with each leg. Then hold the stretch on each side for at least 20 seconds.

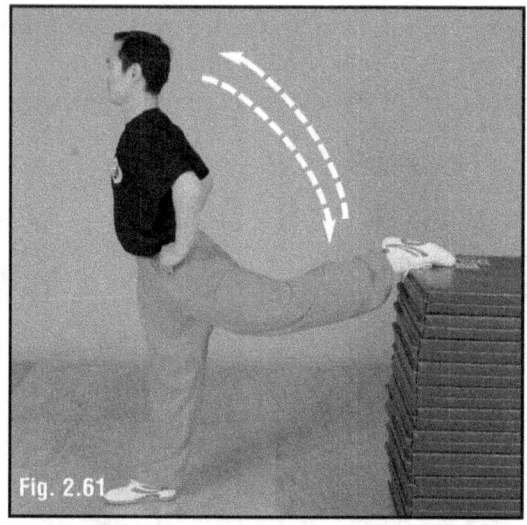

Fig. 2.61

Fig. 2.62

Special Tips: Keep the chest out and the hips squared. Arms can be extended and reaching back to help the body to lean back. Keep the supporting leg straight.

Front Leg Swing (Zheng Bai Tui)

Stand with feet together with one side of your body towards a wall or similar object. Hold to wall with your right hand and extend your left arm outwards, place your left foot behind your body (Fig. 2.63). Start to rhythmically swing your left leg, first forward and up towards the top of your head, and then down and backwards until it reaches its original position (Fig. 2.64 to Fig. 2.66). Repeat the exercise with the other leg.

Fig. 2.63

Fig. 2.64

Fig. 2.65

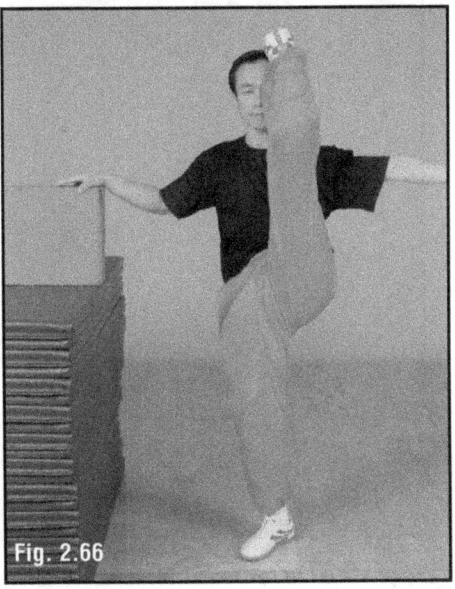

Fig. 2.66

Special Tips: Keep the chest out, the hips squared and the buttocks in. Ankle of the kicking leg should be flexed. Do not lift the heel of the supporting leg.

Side Leg Swing (Ce Bai Tui)

Stand with feet together facing a wall or similar object. Hold to wall with both hands and bring your left leg behind your body (Fig. 2.67). Start to rhythmically swing your left leg up towards the top of your head and then down until it reaches its original position (Fig. 2.68 to Fig. 2.70). Repeat the exercise with the other leg.

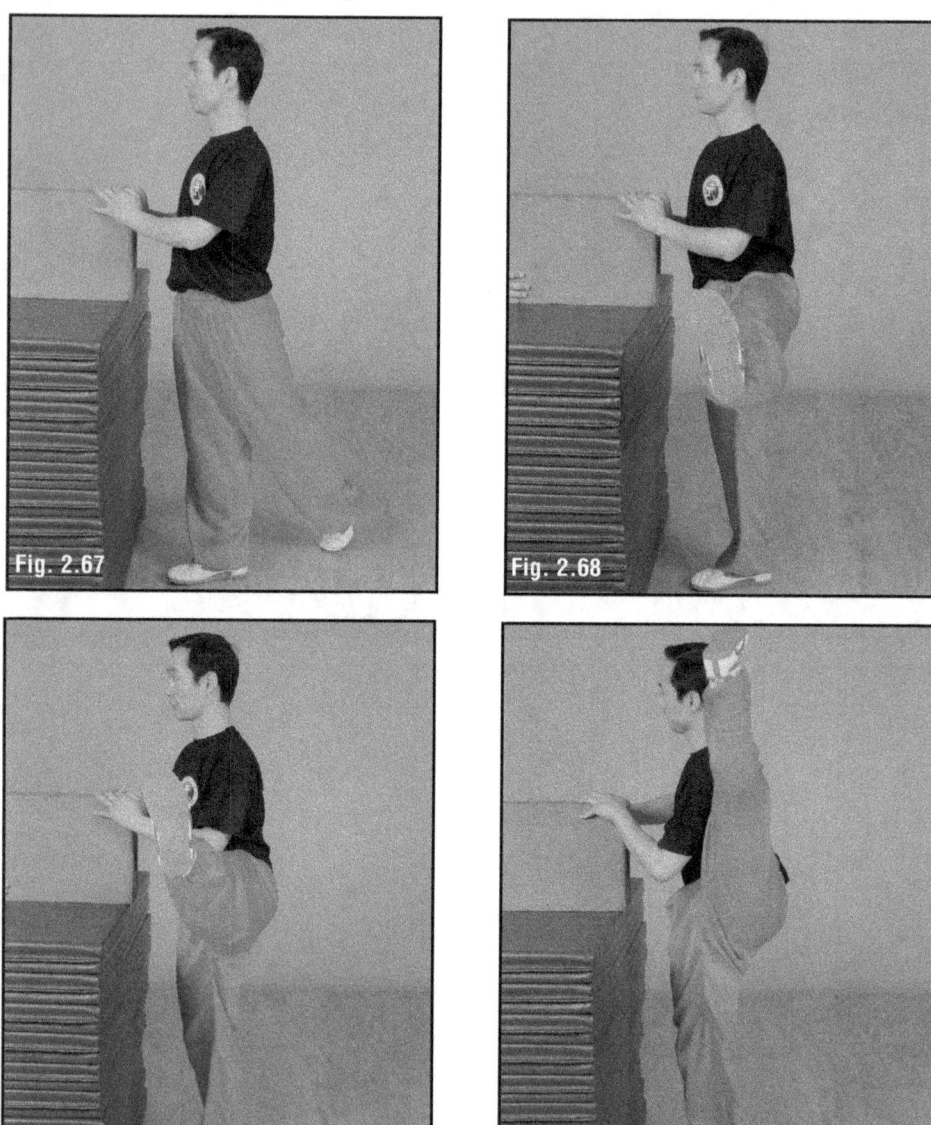

Special Tips: Keep the chest out, the hips squared and the buttocks in. Ankle of the kicking leg should be flexed. Do not lift the heel of the supporting leg.

Back Leg Swing (Hou Bai Tui)

Stand with feet together facing a wall or similar object. Bend your body by the waist, stretch both arms to the front and hold to wall with both hands and bring your left foot a bit forward (Fig. 2.71). Start to rhythmically swing your left leg backwards as high as you can, and then down and front until it reaches its original position (Fig. 2.72 to Fig. 2.74). Repeat the exercise with the other leg.

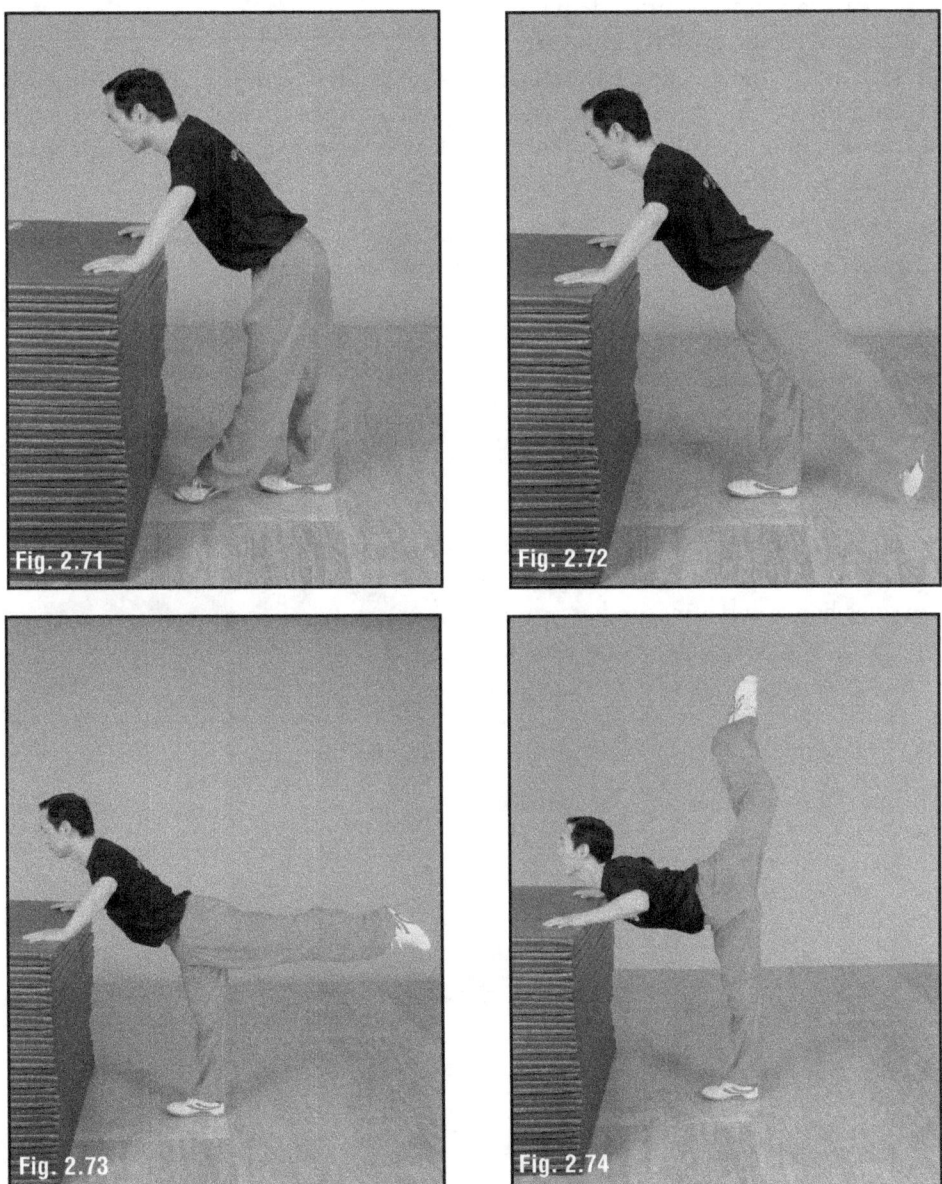

Special Tips: Keep the chest out, the hips squared and the buttocks in. Arch your neck and back while you swing the leg back. Toes of the kicking leg should be pointed. Do not lift the heel of the supporting leg.

Forward Splits (Shu Cha)

Fig. 2.75

Stand with feet together with the arms straight and palms on the sides of your legs. Slide one leg back and bend your other leg at the knee until you can place both hands on the floor. Support your weight on your hands and arms, and continue to slide both legs into a forward splits. The front leg should be facing up with hamstrings and heel supported on the ground, ankle flexed and toes pointing upwards. The back leg should be facing down with the thigh, kneecap and instep supported on the ground, ankle extended and toes pointed. Extend your arms to the sides pushing out with both palms (Fig. 2.75). Repeat the exercise on the opposite side.

Special Tips: Keep the chest out and hips squared. Lower yourself as much as possible into the ground. Alternatively, the back leg can be supported on the inner thigh with the kneecap and foot facing to the side, this is especially recommended when executing split landings from jumps. Hold each stretch at least 30 seconds.

Side Splits (Heng Cha)

Fig. 2.76

Stand with feet together with the arms straight and palms on the sides of your legs. Step out to the side with the right leg at least double shoulder width apart, bend forward and place both hands on the ground between the legs. Support your weight on your hands and arms, and continue to slide both legs into a side splits. Both legs should rest on the inner thigh muscles with kneecaps and insteps facing forward, toes pointed. Keep your upper body upright. Extend your arms to the sides pushing out with both palms (Fig. 2.76).

Special Tips: Keep the chest out. Lower yourself as much as possible into the ground. Hold the stretch at least 30 seconds.

2.2. Hand Forms and Hand Techniques

The hand forms of Wushu refer to the particular shapes of the hands when performing certain hand techniques, which in turn, refer to the movements executed with the hands, forearms, elbows and even with the shoulders. The basic program of Wushu contains three basic hand forms: fist, palm and hook. However, there are many other hand forms such as the single-finger palm, tiger claw, eagle claw, mantis hand, phoenix-eye fist and many more, that are learned as practitioners experiment with other styles of Wushu. The hand techniques of Wushu vary greatly in method and range, both right and left handed techniques are used for attack and defense in all directions. On this section we have twelve of the most common hand techniques including five performed with the fists, five performed with the palms and two performed with the elbows. As you progress through them there are many variations that can be added.

Beginners should pay great attention to the specification of each hand form. It is very common to see fists that are not clenched correctly, loose wrists, palms with opened fingers or with the thumb hanging out. There are many ways to avoid this from happening; for example, you may try to perform pushups with the fists in order to feel the correct position of the fists and wrists. On palms with opened fingers, taping can be used on extreme cases. It is not a bad idea to actually hit a striking bag, understanding and feeling the actual applications of each technique will help you to avoid common mistakes. You may combine hand techniques with stances and footwork practices, which will allow you to eventually grasp the correct method of force generation as well, preparing you to perform hand techniques properly as part of more complex combinations.

Fist (Quan)

Open your hand with your fingers extended and touching each other. Then, separate the thumb and close the four fingers towards the center of the palm with the thumb tightly pressed on the top of the index and the middle fingers (Fig. 2.77). Keep the wrist straight, clench the fingers tight and keep the face of the fist flat.

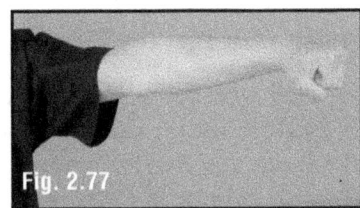

Fig. 2.77

Palm (Zhang)

Open your hand with your fingers extended and touching each other. Then, arch the hand backward and fold the thumb into the palm, bending the top of the thumb downward (Fig. 2.78). Depending on the technique, the wrist could be kept straight, upright or bent 90 degrees backwards.

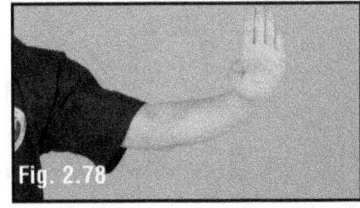

Fig. 2.78

Hook (Gou)

Open your hand with your fingers extended and touching each other. Then, squeeze all the finger tips together to form one tight point and bend the wrist down as much as possible (Fig. 2.79).

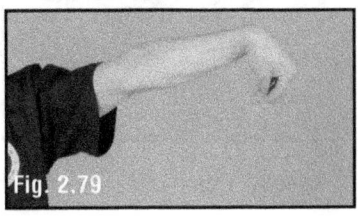

Fig. 2.79

Straight Punch (Chong Quan)

Stand with feet shoulder-width apart with your hands as fists with the palms facing up and pressed against the sides at waist level (Fig. 2.80). Thrust your fist out in a straight line, twisting the forearm inward just before impact so that the palm is facing down or inwards in case of a vertical punch. Look to the front (Fig. 2.81). Repeat the exercise with the other arm (Fig. 2.82).

Fig. 2.80

Fig. 2.81

Fig. 2.82

Special Tips: Force should be applied on the face of the fist. Increase speed and power by twisting the hips, shifting the center of gravity forward and driving the shoulder of the striking arm out. The punch should be delivered at shoulder level.

Downward Fist (Pi Quan)

Stand with feet shoulder-width apart with your hands as fists with the palms facing up and pressed against the sides at waist level (Fig. 2.83). Raise the right fist up with the arm straight over the head (Fig. 2.84). Execute a downward hammer-like motion and bring your left palm close to the arm in front of your chest. Look to the front (Fig. 2.85). Repeat the exercise with the other arm.

Fig. 2.83

Fig. 2.84

Fig. 2.85

Special Tips: Relax the shoulders. Force should be applied on the wheel of the fist.

Overhead Fist (Guan Quan)

Stand with feet shoulder-width apart with your hands as fists with the palms facing up and pressed against the sides at waist level (Fig. 2.86). Lean your body the left and swing your right arm obliquely upwards in an arc in front of the body. Lift the left arm and open the fist into a palm facing. Strike the back of the right fist on your left palm to the left over your head. Follow the right fist with your eyes (Fig. 2.87). Repeat exercise with the other arm.

Fig. 2.86

Fig. 2.87

Special Tips: Relax the shoulders. Both elbows should be slightly bent.

Reverse Fist (Heng Quan)

Stand with feet shoulder-width apart with your hands as fists with the palms facing up and pressed against the sides at waist level (Fig. 2.88). Open your left fist into a palm and extend your left arm straight out towards the left side of your body, palm facing forward. At the same time, bend right arm by the elbow and bring your right fist up and left towards the left side of your chest, palm of the fist faces your body. Look to the left (Fig. 2.89). Swing your right arm horizontally and strike with the back of your fist to the right of your body with the arm straight. Left palm moves to the right simultaneously, elbow bent, palm covers the right side of your chest facing to the right. Follow the right fist with your eyes (Fig. 2.90). Repeat exercise with the other arm.

Fig. 2.88

Fig. 2.89

Fig. 2.90

Special Tips: Relax the shoulders. Force should be applied on the back of the fist.

Hammer Fist (Za Quan)

Stand with feet together with your hands as fists with the palms facing up and pressed against the sides at waist level (Fig. 2.91). Raise the right arm straight over your head and lift the right knee, bring the left arm to the side of the body, bent the elbow and open the fist into a palm facing down (Fig. 2.92). Swing your right arm forward and downward in an arc, bring your left palm up and strike it with the back of your right fist in front of your waist at the same time that you

Fig. 2.91

Fig. 2.92

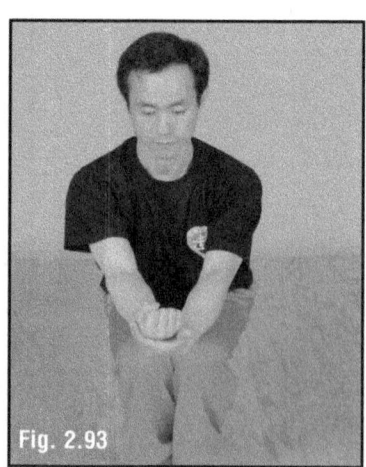
Fig. 2.93

bring your right foot down near your left foot and stomp on the ground while bending both legs to a half squat with feet together. Look to the right fist (Fig. 2.93).

Special Tips: Keep the chest out and relax the shoulders. Turn the right forearm inward as you swing your right arm down. Force should be applied on the back of the fist. Foot stomp and hammer fist strike must be done at the same time.

Pushing Palm (Tui Zhang)

Stand with feet shoulder-width apart with your hands as palms pressed against the sides at waist level. Both palms face forward while the fingers point to the ground (Fig. 2.94). Thrust your palm out in a straight line, twisting the forearm inward just before impact so that the fingers of the palm are pointing up. Look to the right palm (Fig. 2.95). Repeat the exercise with the other arm (Fig. 2.96).

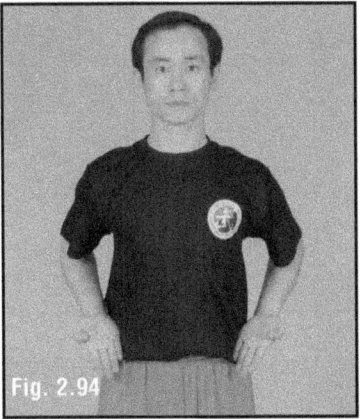

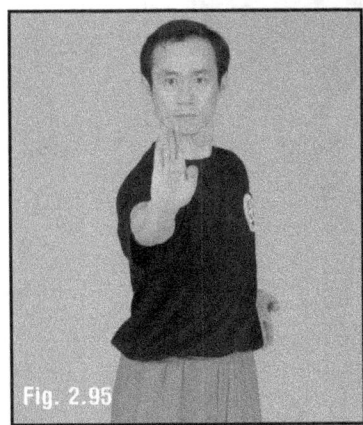

Special Tips: Force should be applied on the outer edge of the palm. Increase speed and power by twisting the hips, shifting the center of gravity forward and driving the shoulder of the striking arm out. The palm strike should be delivered at shoulder level.

Flashing Palm (Liang Zhang)

Stand with feet shoulder-width apart with your hands as palms facing up and pressed against the sides at waist level (Fig. 2.97). Open your left fist into a palm and swing your left arm in an arc out and up. Look to the left (Fig. 2.98). As you reach the vertical line with your arm, snap the wrist inward and place the palm upright. Look to the right (Fig. 2.99). Repeat the exercise with the other arm.

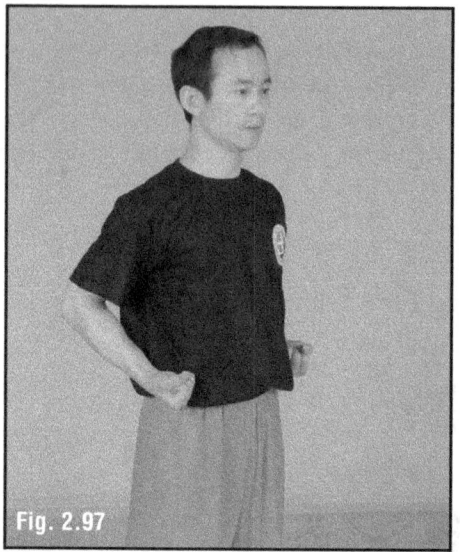

Special Tips: Relax the shoulders. Force should be applied on the fingers tips. Snap the wrist and turn the head at the same time.

Threading Palm (Chuan Zhang)

Stand with feet shoulder-width apart with your hands as fists with the palms facing up and pressed against the sides at waist level (Fig 2.100). Swing your left arm in an arc to the left side of your body (Fig 2.101). Continue the arc up over your head and down in front of your face until it reaches the right side of the body at shoulder level. Turn your waist slightly to the right (Fig 2.102). Open your right fist into a palm and thrust the palm out while threading with your fingers near the top of your left palm. The right palm should face up. Look to the threading palm (Fig 2.103). Repeat the exercise with the other arm.

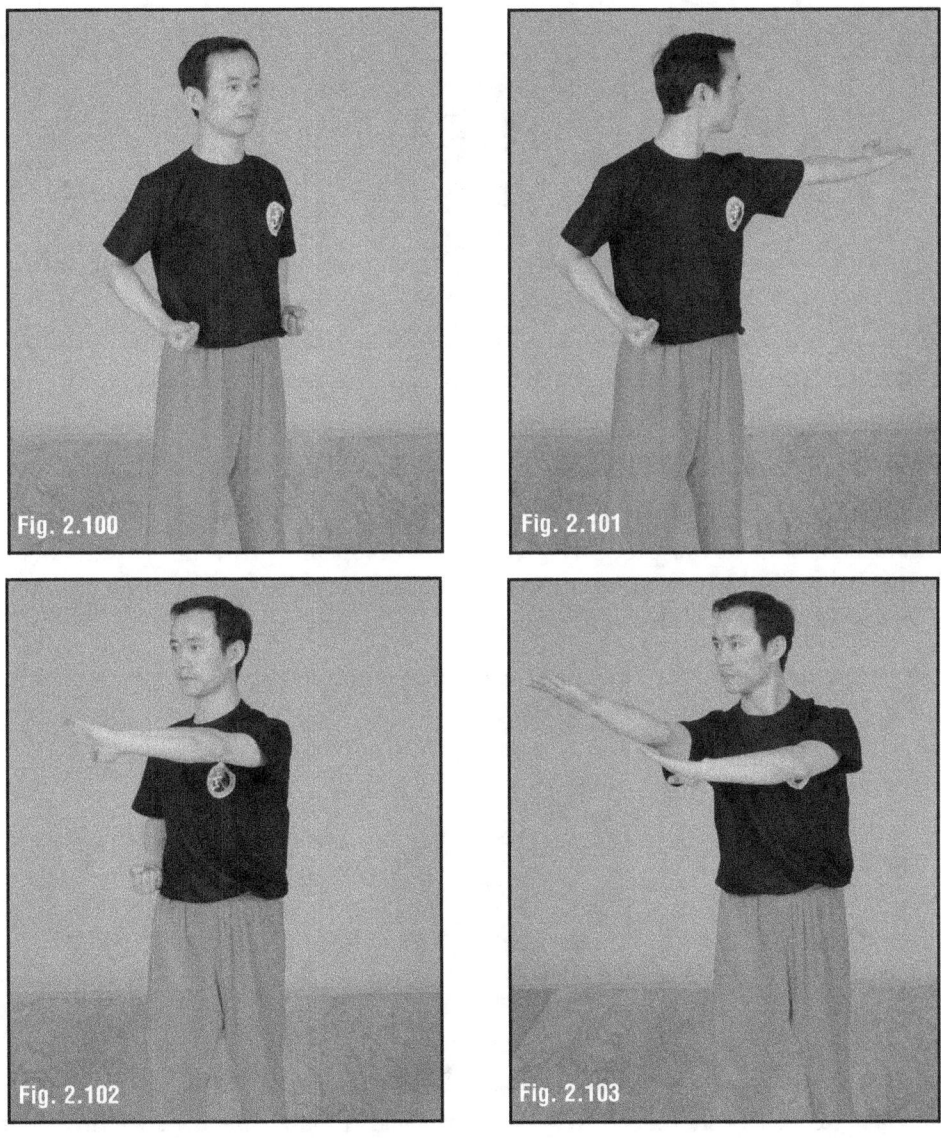

Special Tips: Relax the shoulders. Keep palm facing up. Force should be applied to the finger tips. Thrust should be delivered at face level

Downward Chop (Pi Zhang)

Stand with feet shoulder-width apart with your hands as fists with the palms facing up and pressed against the sides at waist level (Fig 2.104). Open your right fist into a palm and raise the right arm up. Open your left fist into a palm and let you arm naturally hang on the left side of your body (Fig 2.105). Execute a downward slashing motion and bring your left palm close to the arm in front of your chest. Look to the front (Fig 2.106). Repeat the exercise with the other arm.

Special Tips: Relax the shoulders. Keep palm vertical. Force should be applied in the outer edge of the palm.

Up-Swinging Palm (Liao Zhang)

Stand with feet shoulder-width apart with your hands as fists with the palms facing up and pressed against the sides at waist level (Fig 2.107). Form a palm with your right arm and swing it upwards from below (Fig 2.108). Snap the wrist and place the palm upright. Look to the front (Fig 2.109). Repeat the exercise with the other arm.

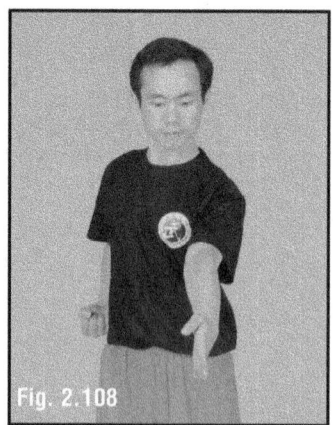

Special Tips: Relax the shoulders. Keep palm vertical. Elbow should be slightly bent. Force should be applied in the outer edge of the palm.

Thrusting Elbow (Ding Zhou)

Stand with feet shoulder-width apart with your hands as fists with the palms facing up and pressed against the sides at waist level (Fig 2.110). Open your right fist into a palm and raise your right arm to the right side of your body at shoulder level, bring your left arm in front of your chest, keep the elbow bent and the left fist with the palm facing down in front of the right side of your chest (Fig 2.111). Move your right arm to the left so the right palm meets with the left fist. Strike with the right elbow towards the right side of the body. Look to the same direction of the elbow thrust (Fig 2.112). Repeat the exercise with the other arm.

Fig. 2.110

Fig. 2.111

Fig. 2.112

Special Tips: Relax the shoulders. Reach out with the elbow. Support arm should stay in contact with the torso and the force should be directed on the tip of the elbow.

Bending Elbow (Pan Zhou)

Stand with feet shoulder-width apart with your hands as fists with the palms facing up and pressed against the sides at waist level (Fig 2.113). Perform a circular movement with your right arm striking with your elbow in front of your body. Look to the same direction of the elbow strike (Fig 2.114). Repeat the exercise with the other arm.

Special Tips: Relax the shoulders. Increase the speed by rotating the hips and shoulders to drive the elbow across the front of the body. Force should be directed on the tip of the elbow.

Fig. 2.113

Fig. 2.114

2.3. Stances and Footwork

The stances of Wushu are comprised of a series of static postures that represent the base of support of the practitioner to the ground. Apart from being the platform for all Wushu techniques, stances are aimed to increase leg strength and improve the flexibility of the hips, legs and ankles. Footwork in Wushu is concerned with the different ways of stepping, leaping or shifting from one stance to another. On this section we have included seven stances and five types of footwork and as you progress through them there are many variations that can be added.

Beginners may start by understanding the requirements of each stance. For example, you can assume a high horse stance first and gradually go lower to feel the tension in your thighs and lower back. Play with different heights and turn your waist from side to side to notice how the tension differs and identify the areas you need to work upon and finally grasp the mechanics behind each stance. In terms of footwork, beginners should familiarize with each stepping pattern keeping in mind that the main purpose is to be able to ensure that the body is centered and controlled at all times while moving forward, backward, left, right and when pivoting in general.

Practice your stances and footwork diligently and regularly. The most common stance training consists of choosing a sequence of stances and holding them for periods of 10 to 30 seconds each. This will give you the opportunity to check the correctness of each stance, as well as the way you transition from one stance into another. Learn how to measure your progress and make sure you have the necessary strength and flexibility to be able to go down on your stances without over stressing on your joints, ligaments and tendons of your legs. After diligent practice, you will be able to hold properly executed stances for several minutes without discomfort.

Keep in mind that incorrect technique on your stances such as letting your knee go past your toes when doing a bow stance, opening your supporting foot outwards and bending your knee inwards when doing drop stance or empty stance, and others postural problems could have serious repercussions after year of practice. Inefficient stances, whether by mistake, lack of foundation or to incorrectly try to enhance their external appearance, once they become habitual they will cause adaptive responses from your leg muscles, tendons and ligaments which could eventually lead to injury. A general rule is keep your toes aligned with your knees at all times. Once again, flexibility, strength and correct technique must go hand in hand in order to avoid injury.

Bow Stance (Gong Bu)

Take a step forward of about five times the length of your foot. Bend the front leg to a half squat position having the shin perpendicular to the ground and the thigh parallel to the ground forming a 90 degree angle at the knee. Look to the front. Front view (Fig 2.115). Side view (Fig 2.116).

Fig. 2.115

Fig. 2.116

Special Tips: Keep the body upright, hips squared and chest out. The back leg is straight. Both feet should be flat on the ground.

Horse Stance (Ma Bu)

Take a step sideways of about three times the length of your foot. Hips are squared and feet should remain parallel with toes pointing forward. Bend both legs to a half squat position having both shins perpendicular to the ground and thighs parallel to the ground forming a 90 degree angle at both knees. Look to the front. Front view (Fig 2.117). Side view (Fig 2.118).

Special Tips: Keep the body upright, chest out and buttocks in. Weight is centered. Both feet should be flat on the ground.

Fig. 2.117

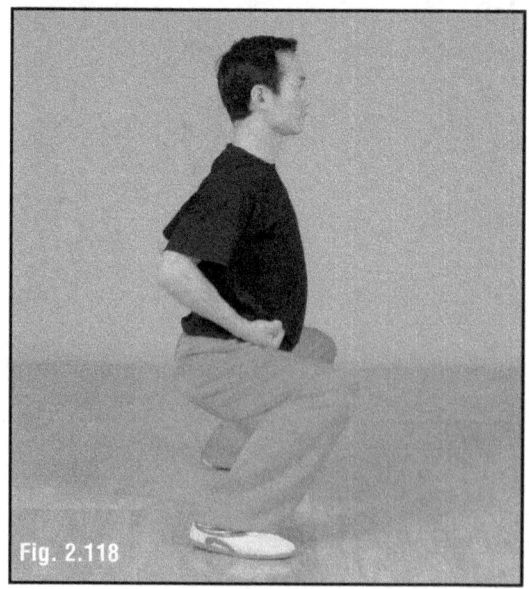
Fig. 2.118

Empty Stance (Xu Bu)

Raise one leg and turn the foot of the supporting leg 45 degrees outwards. Bend the supporting leg to a half squat position and place the raised leg forward about two times the length of your foot. Toes of front leg must be pointed and lightly positioned on the ground. The thigh of the front leg should be parallel to the ground. Back foot should be flat on the ground. Front view (Fig 2.119). Side view (Fig 2.120).

Special Tips: Keep the body upright, chest out and buttocks in. Toes of bent leg should point outwards no more than 45 degrees.

Fig. 2.119

Fig. 2.120

Drop Stance (Pu Bu)

Take a step sideways of about five times the length of your foot and place your foot flat on the ground, toes pointing forward and leg straight. Bend your supporting leg to a complete squat, touching the thigh on the calf and bringing your buttocks as low as possible. Look to the side of the extended leg. Front view (Fig 2.121). Side view (Fig 2.122).

Special Tips: Keep the body upright, chest out and buttocks in. Both feet should remain flat on the ground. Toes of bent leg should point outwards no more than 45 degrees. Toes of straight leg should point forward.

Fig. 2.121

Fig. 2.122

Resting Stance (Xie Bu)

Place one leg one step in front of the other leg. Turn your body to the side of your front leg and cross the legs into a full squat position resting on the back leg. Look to the side of the front leg. Front view (Fig 2.123). Side view (Fig 2.124).

Special Tips: Keep the body upright, chest out and buttocks in. Both legs are tightly against each other, the foot of the front leg is flat on the ground with toes pointing out, the back heel is raised and the buttocks sit on the calf near the heel.

Fig. 2.123

Fig. 2.124

Sitting Stance (Zuo Pan)

Take a step sideways of about three times the length of your foot. Bring your center of gravity down as you turn your body pivoting with both feet. As you turn, your legs will naturally form a crossed stance until you sit down on the ground. Direction of the eyes is optional depending on the arms position. Front view (Fig 2.125). Side view (Fig 2.126).

Special Tips: Keep the body upright and chest out. Both legs are tightly against each other, the foot of the front leg is supported on the outer edge and points outwards. The foot of the back leg is turned in and supported on the instep.

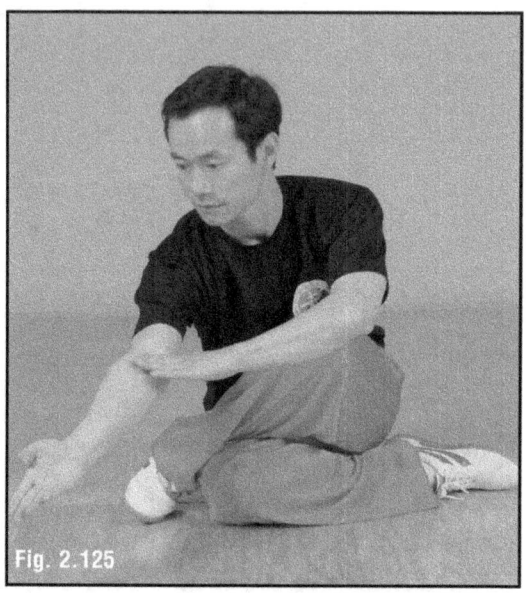
Fig. 2.125

Fig. 2.126

T Stance (Ding Bu)

Raise one leg and bend the supporting leg to a half squat. Place the raised foot again on the ground slightly backwards from its original position forming a "T" shape in relation to the supporting foot. Place only the toes or the ball of the foot as you lower your center of gravity. Look to the side of the raised leg. Front view (Fig 2.127). Side view (Fig 2.128).

Special Tips: Keep the body upright, chest out and buttocks in. Supporting foot should be flat on the ground.

Fig. 2.127

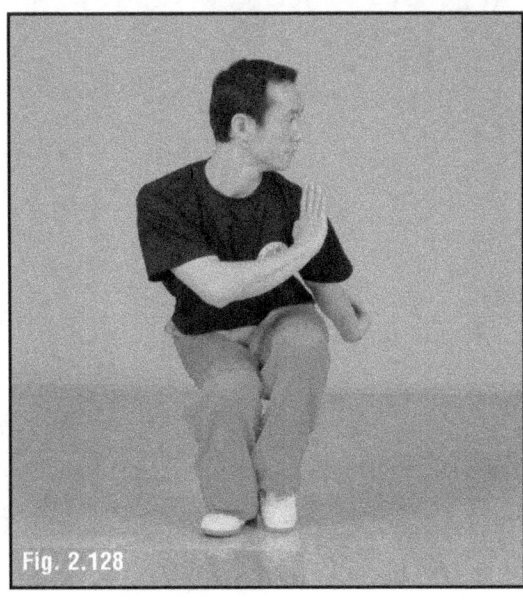

Fig. 2.128

Forward Step (Xing Bu)

Assume a right high empty stance with the right arm straight over the head and the left palm pressed on the left side of the waist (Fig. 2.129). Step with your left foot first and swing your left arm forward in an arc. Each step slightly bigger then shoulder width along a curved line. Extend your right arm to the right side of the body (Fig. 2.130 to Fig. 2.133). Repeat the exercise in the opposite direction.

Fig. 2.129

Fig. 2.130

Fig. 2.131

Fig. 2.132

Fig. 2.133

Special Tips: When making a circle to the left, the toes of the left foot turn outwards and the toes of the right foot turn inwards. When making a circle to the right, the toes of the left foot turn inwards and the toes of the right foot turn outwards. Keep the upper body at the same level, the head should remain at the same height through the whole pattern.

Front Crossed Step (Gai Bu)

Stand with feet shoulder-width apart with your hands as fists with the palms facing up and pressed against the sides at waist level (Fig. 2.134). Cross your right leg over your left leg. Turn the toes of the stepping foot outward and place it in front and across the body to form a crossed step (Fig. 2.135).

Fig. 2.134 Fig. 2.135

Special Tips: Keep the body upright and chest out. Lift the heel of the left leg and the left knee can be slightly bent.

Back Crossed Step (Cha Bu)

Stand with feet shoulder-width apart with your hands as fists with the palms facing up and pressed against the sides at waist level (Fig. 2.136). Cross your left leg behind your right leg. Turn the toes of the front foot outward while placing the back foot behind and across the body to form a crossed step. (Fig. 2.137)

Fig. 2.136 Fig. 2.137

Special Tips: Keep the body upright and chest out. Lift the heel of the left leg and keep the left knee straight.

Tapping Step (Ji Bu)

As you run forward, extend your left arm to the front and the right arm to the back (Fig 2.138). Cross your right foot over and push off with both feet to drive the body forward and upward at the same time while your circle both arms in front of your body. Quickly tap the heel of leading foot with the inner side of the rear foot as you extend your arms again in midair (Fig 2.139 to Fig. 2.141).

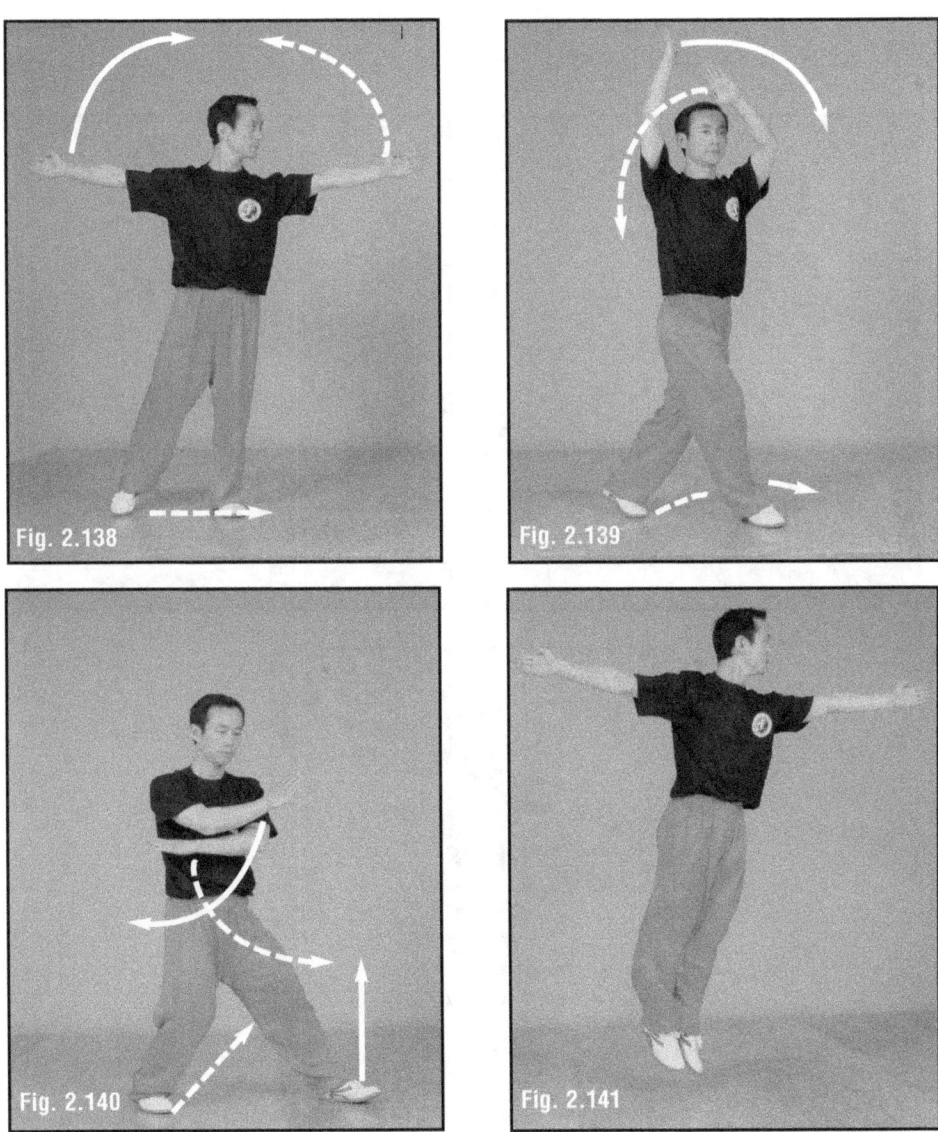

Fig. 2.138   Fig. 2.139
Fig. 2.140   Fig. 2.141

Special Tips: All movements should be performed in one single motion. Land with the rear foot first and continue into the next movement without loosing any speed.

Giant Leap and Swing Palm (Da Yue Bu Qian Chuan)

As you run forward, make a step with your right foot, left knee slightly bent, turn your trunk to the left and move your left arm backwards while you swing the right arm forward and place it in front of the raised knee (Fig 2.142). Step forward with your left foot and bend body slightly forward as you to prepare to jump (Fig 2.143). Jump forcefully while swinging your right arm forward and upward. Turn your body to the right and lift your right knee first. As you are in midair, continue the natural circle with your arms so that the right arm presses back with the palm and your left arms presses up with the palm, the right leg is straighten and the left is kept bent by the knee and pressed backwards with toes pointed (Fig 2.144).

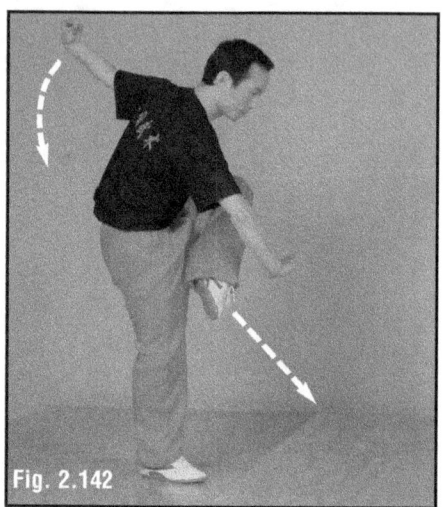
Fig. 2.142

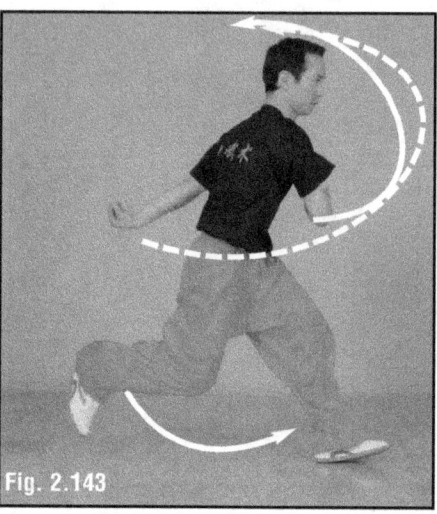
Fig. 2.143

Fig. 2.144

Special Tips: All movements should be performed in one single motion. Arms should swing on a vertical plain and eyes should follow the right palm. Land with the right foot first and continue naturally into the next movement.

2.4. Leg Techniques

The leg techniques of Wushu consist of a series of movements with the legs that vary greatly in method and application. Some of them are practiced as a complement to the leg stretching exercises shown on previous sections of this book, while others are actual kicks delivered to imaginary targets. In general, leg techniques are classified in two main groups: straight leg kicks and bent leg kicks. As the name implies, kicks in which the leg is straight through the entire movement belong to the first group, while the latter involves kicks delivered by bending the leg by the knee and snapping it to full extension. On this section we have included twelve of the major leg techniques of Wushu and as you progress through them there are many variations that can be added.

Beginners should pay special attention to the basic requirements and correct execution of each leg technique through practice. For example, while learning the front stretch kick some may consider that kicking over the head is a great accomplishment; however, this is not the case since the specifications of the movement require the practitioner to aim to his forehead with the kicking foot. Therefore, the emphasis must be placed upon the correct body posture and alignment when kicking. Remember that wrong posture, once it becomes a habit, is very hard to correct.

Lastly, all actual kick techniques require expressing the power of the kick through a specific area of the foot, and as with hand techniques, it is not a bad idea to actually kick a striking bag. Understanding the actual applications of each technique will always help you to avoid common mistakes. As you advance and refine your leg techniques in general, you will notice how your jumping techniques will also improve greatly.

Front Stretch Kick (Zheng Ti Tui)

Stand with feet together with arms extended to the sides at shoulder level and hands extended in palms, look to front (Fig. 2.145). Take a step forward with the right foot (Fig. 2.146). Shift your weight forward and kick forcefully the left leg straight up pointing the toes towards the forehead (Fig. 2.147). Bring the leg down fast and place your right foot in its original position (Fig. 2.148). Repeat the exercise with the other leg.

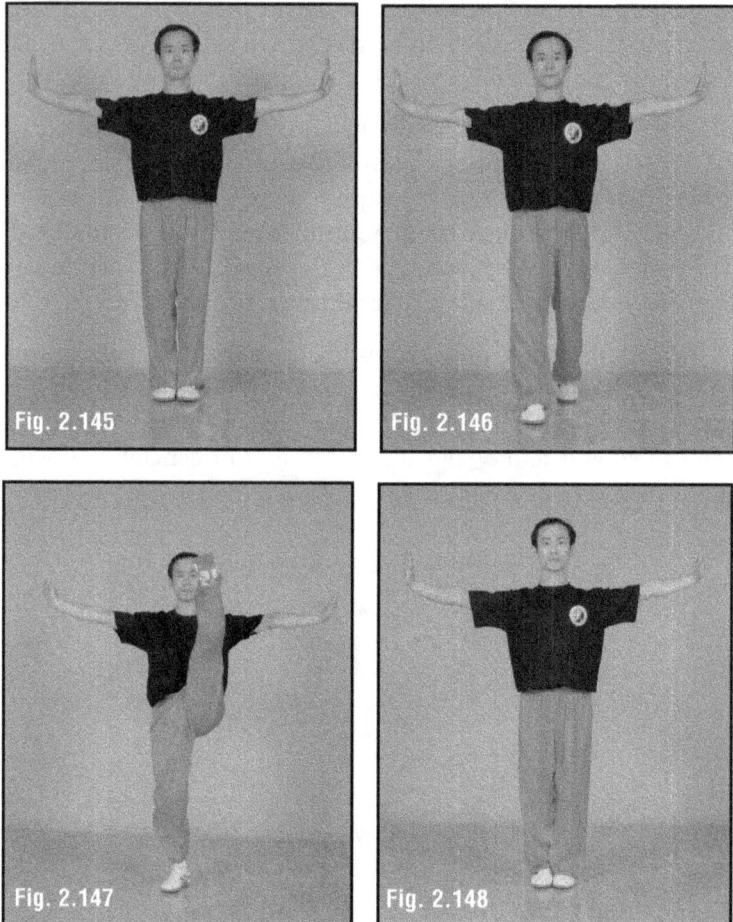

Special Tips: Keep the chest out and the hips squared. The kicking leg must be straight through the whole movement and the ankle flexed. The foot of the supporting leg should be flat on the ground (Fig 2.149).

Side Stretch Kick (Ce Ti Tui)

Stand sideways with feet together, look to your left side, extend your left arm to the front and the right arm to the back, both hands extended in palms (Fig 2.150). Take a step obliquely forward with the right foot (Fig. 2.151). Shift your weight forward and kick forcefully the left leg straight up pointing the toes towards the side of your head. Bend your left arm by the elbow and place your left palm in front of your right armpit and raise your right palm over your head. Look to the front (Fig. 2.152). Bring the leg down fast and place your left foot in its original position. Look to your left side and extend the arms again to their original position (Fig. 2.153). Repeat the exercise with the other leg.

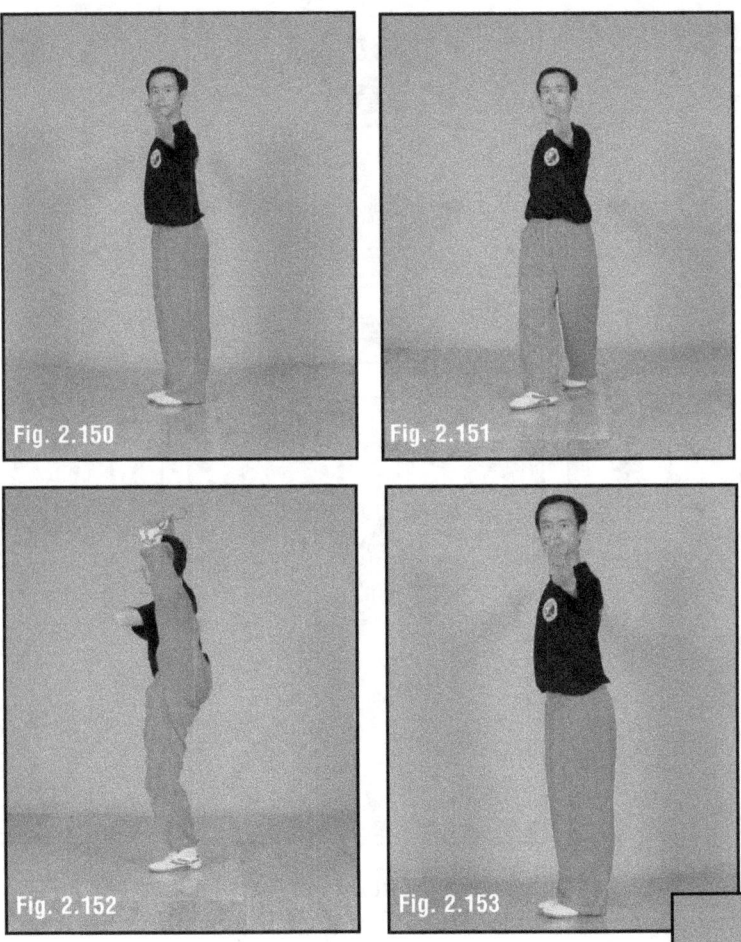

Fig. 2.150

Fig. 2.151

Fig. 2.152

Fig. 2.153

Fig. 2.154 - front view

Special Tips: Keep the body upright and the chest out. The kicking leg must be straight through the whole movement and the ankle flexed. Foot of supporting leg should be flat on the ground (Fig 2.154).

Inside Stretch Kick (Li He Tui)

Stand with feet together with arms extended to the sides at shoulder level and hands extended in palms, look to the front (Fig. 2.155). Take a step obliquely forward (Fig. 2.156). Kick your right leg forcefully up in an arc. The leg goes outwards, up, crosses the face and then inwards and down (Fig 2.157 to Fig. 2.159). Bring the leg down fast and place your right foot in its original position (Fig. 2.160). Repeat the exercise with the other leg.

Fig. 2.155

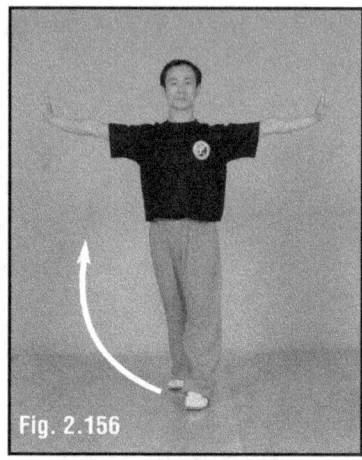
Fig. 2.156

Fig. 2.157

Fig. 2.158

Fig. 2.159

Fig. 2.160

Special Tips: Keep the body upright and the chest out. The kicking leg must be straight through the whole movement and the ankle flexed. The foot of supporting leg should be flat on the ground.

Outside Stretch Kick (Wai Bai Tui)

Stand with feet together with arms extended to the sides at shoulder level and hands extended in palms, look to the front (Fig. 2.161). Take a step obliquely forward with the left foot (Fig. 2.162). Kick your right leg forcefully up in an arc. The leg goes slightly inwards, up, crosses the face and swings out as wide as possible and down (Fig 2.163 to Fig. 2.165). Bring the leg down fast and place your right foot in its original position (Fig 2.166). Repeat the exercise with the other leg.

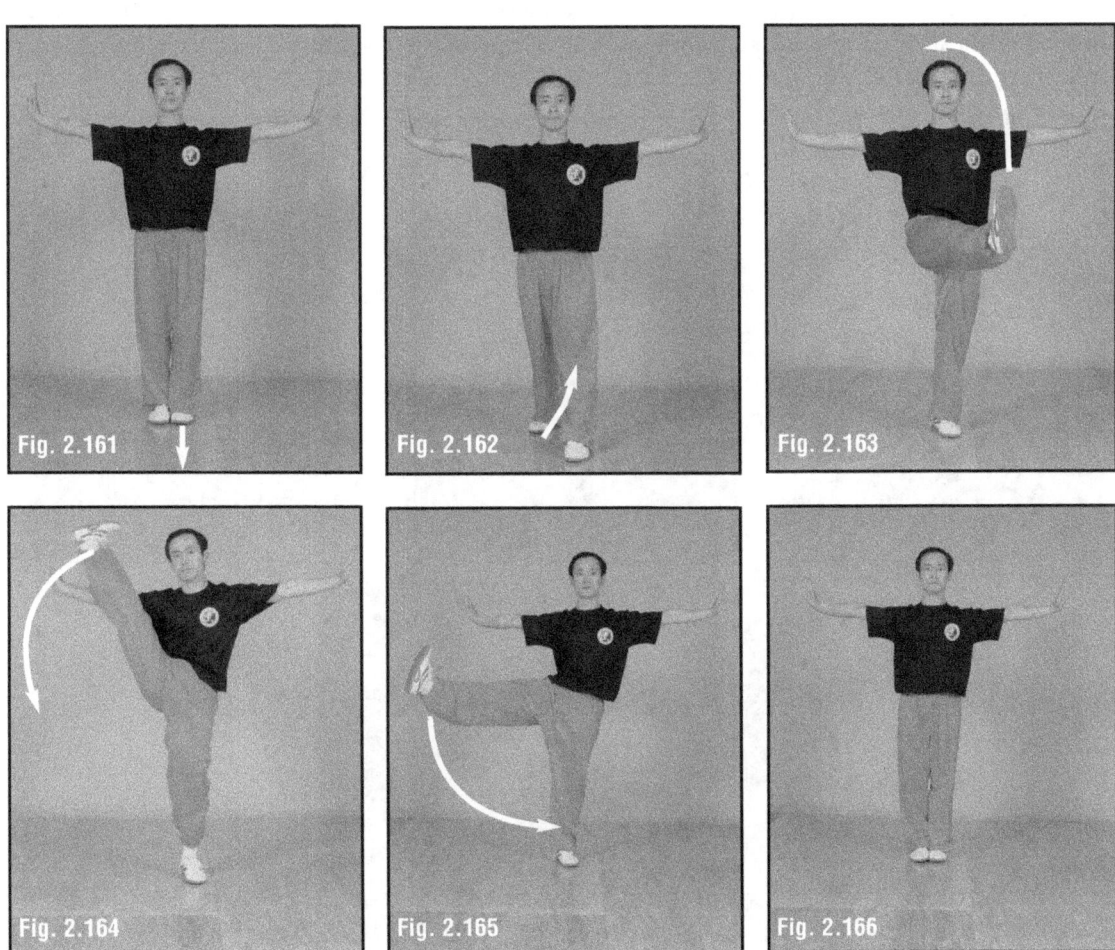

Special Tips: Keep the body upright and the chest out. The kicking leg must be straight through the whole movement and the ankle flexed. The foot of supporting leg should be flat on the ground.

Front Slap Kick (Dan Pai Jiao)

Stand with feet together with arms straight on the sides your body (Fig 2.167). Take a step forward with the left foot (Fig 2.168). Raise left arm over the head with palm facing to the front and following this movement raise your right arm in front of your face with the palm also facing forward (Fig 2.169). Kick forcefully your right leg straight and up towards your face with the instep. As the foot approaches your palms, clap with your left palm into the back of your right palm, immediately after, clap with your right palm into the instep of your right foot at face level. At the moment of the second clap, the left arm should be straighten and positioned on the far left side of the body, palm facing to the left (Fig 2.170). Bring the leg down fast and place your right foot in its original position (Fig 2.171).

Fig. 2.167

Fig. 2.168

Fig. 2.169

Fig. 2.170

Fig. 2.171

Special Tips: Keep the body upright and the chest out. The kicking leg must be straight through the whole movement and the toes pointed. The foot of supporting leg should be flat on the ground. Slap must be accurate, clean and loud.

Inside Slap Kick (Li He Pai Jiao)

Stand with feet together with arms extended to the sides at shoulder level and hands extended in palms, look to the front (Fig. 2.172). Take a step obliquely forward with the left foot (Fig. 2.173). Kick your right leg forcefully up in an arc. The leg goes outward and up (Fig 2.174). The left palm slaps the sole of the right foot after it crosses in front of the face (Fig 2.175). The leg continues the arc going inwards and down (Fig 2.176). Bring the leg down fast and place your right foot in its original position (Fig. 2.177). Repeat the exercise with the other leg.

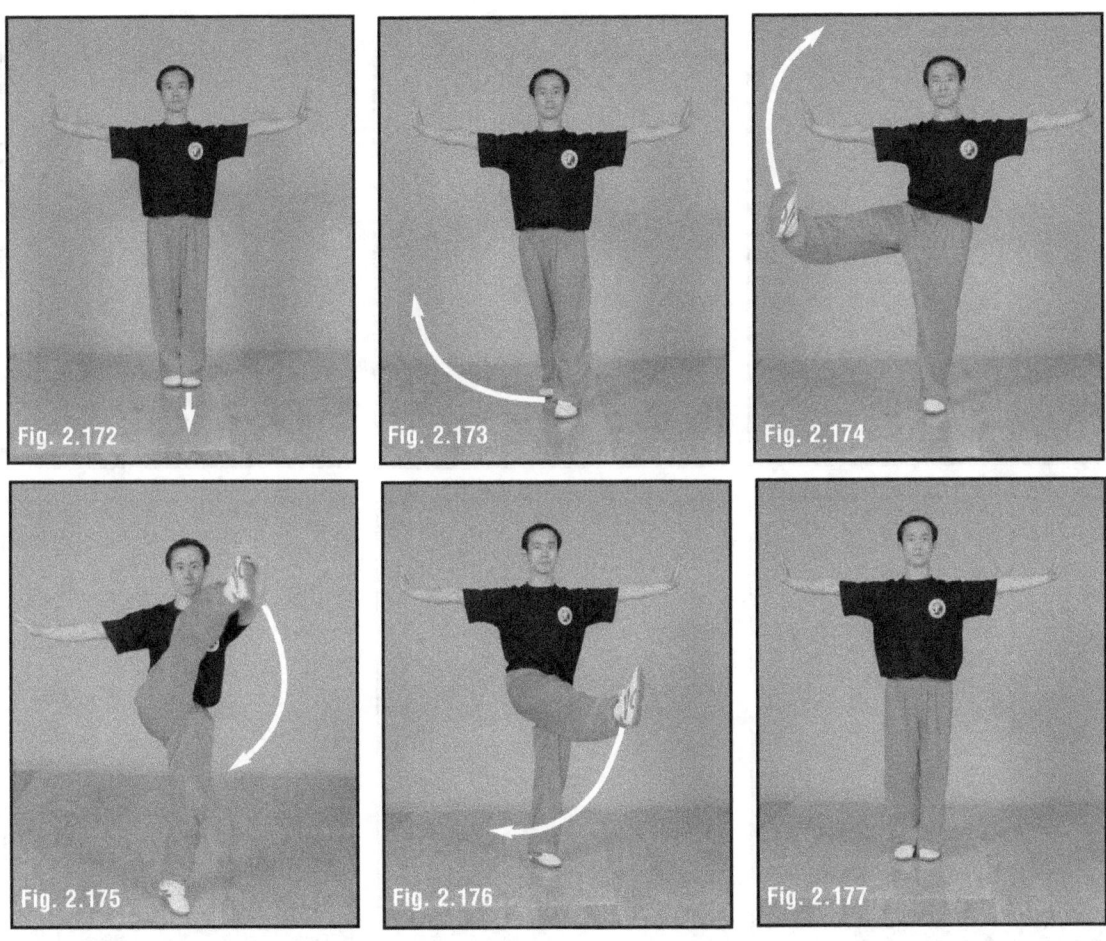

Special Tips: Keep the body upright and the chest out. The kicking leg must be straight through the whole movement and the ankle flexed obliquely inward. The foot of supporting leg should be flat on the ground. Slap must be clean and loud.

Mastering Wushu

Outside Slap Kick (Wai Bai Pai Jiao)

Stand with feet together with arms extended to the sides at shoulder level and hands extended in palms, look to the front (Fig. 2.178). Take a step obliquely forward with the left foot (Fig. 2.179). Kick your right leg forcefully up in an arc. The leg goes slightly inwards and up (Fig. 2.180). Both hands slap the instep of the foot as it crosses in front of the face (Fig. 2.181). The leg swings out as wide as possible and down (Fig 2.182). Bring the leg down fast and place your right foot in its original position (Fig 2.183). Repeat the exercise with the other leg.

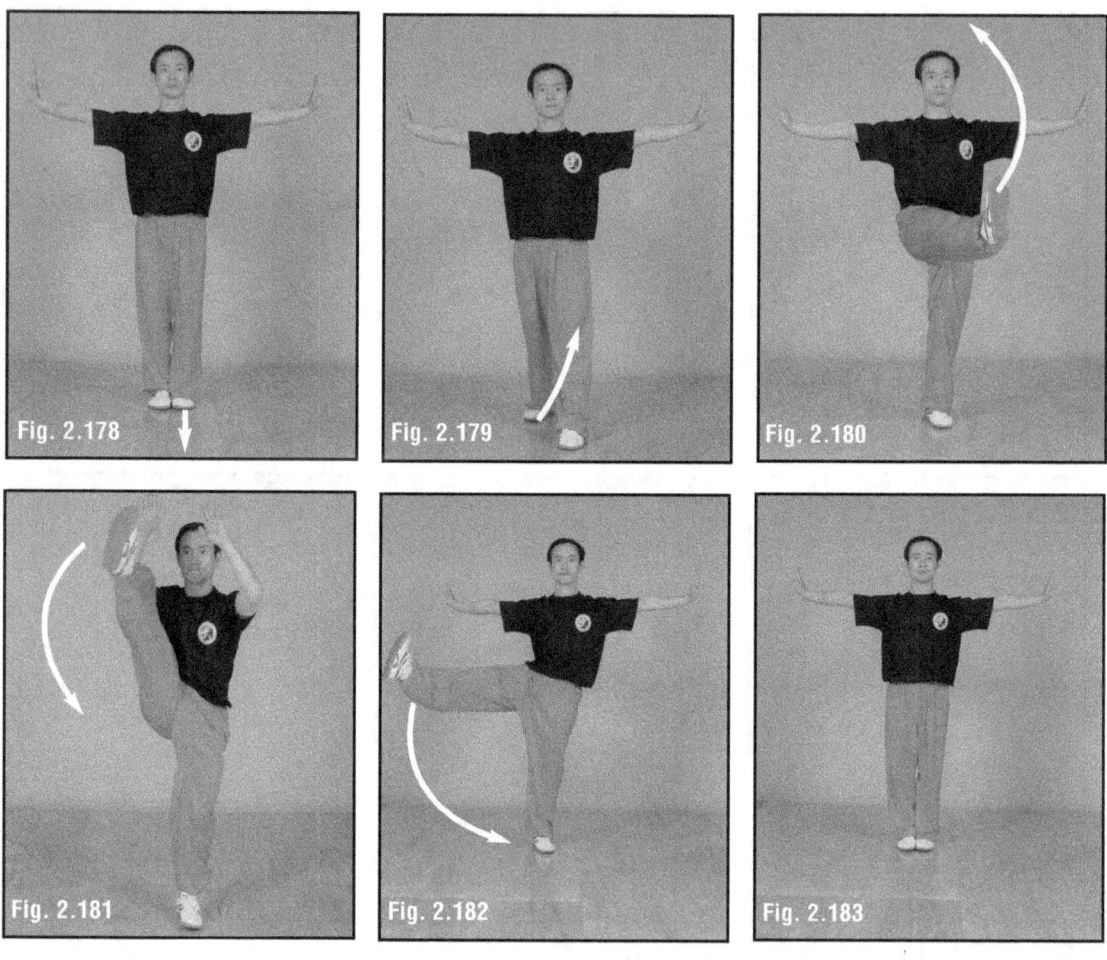

Special Tips: Keep the body upright and the chest out. The kicking leg must be straight through the whole movement and the ankle flexed obliquely inward. The foot of supporting leg should be flat on the ground. Slap must be clean and loud.

Front Snap Kick (Tan Tui)

Stand with feet shoulder-width apart with your hands as fists with the palms facing up and pressed against the sides at waist level (Fig. 2.184). Take a step forward with the left foot (Fig. 2.185). Kick forcefully your right leg by lifting your knee first (Fig. 2.186) and snapping the knee out to full extension kicking with the instep (Fig. 2.187). Bring the leg down fast and place your right foot in front of your body (Fig. 2.188). Repeat the exercise with the other leg.

Fig. 2.184

Fig. 2.185

Fig. 2.186

Fig. 2.187

Fig. 2.188

Special Tips: Keep the body upright and the chest out. The supporting leg should be straight or bent slightly. The power of the kick should be expressed through the toe (Fig 2.189). The foot of supporting leg should be flat on the ground.

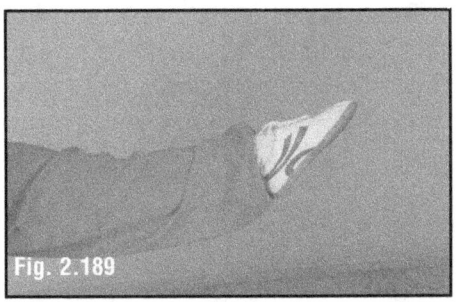
Fig. 2.189

Front Heel Kick (Deng Tui)

Stand with feet shoulder-width apart with your hands as fists with the palms facing up and pressed against the sides at waist level (Fig. 2.190). Take a step forward with the left foot (Fig. 2.191). Kick forcefully your right leg by lifting your knee first (Fig. 2.192) and snapping the knee out to full extension kicking with the heel (Fig. 2.193). Bring the leg down fast and place your right foot in front of your body (Fig. 2.194). Repeat the exercise with the other leg.

Special Tips: Keep the body upright and the chest out. The supporting leg should be straight or bent slightly. The power of the kick should be expressed through the heel (Fig 2.195). The foot of supporting leg should be flat on the ground.

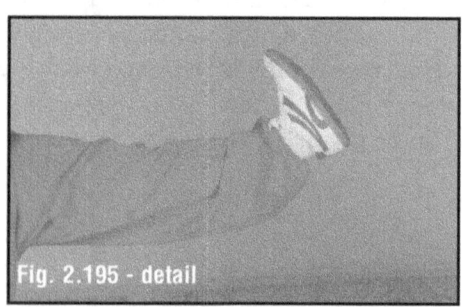

Side Kick (Ce Chuai Tui)

Stand with feet shoulder-width apart with your hands as fists with the palms facing up and pressed against the sides at waist level (Fig. 2.196). Perform a front crossed step with the right leg and at the same time cross both arms in front of the body, right palm over the left palm with the elbows bent at chest level (Fig. 2.197). Stand on the right foot and raise your left leg bringing the knee as high as possible, chamber the hip and keep the shin parallel to the ground and the sole of the foot pointing at your target. Open your right foot clockwise between 45 to 90 degrees and thrust your left leg forcefully, extend both arms to the sides and push with the palms (Fig. 2.198). Bring the leg down by coiling the knee first and placing your left foot on the left side of your right foot. Repeat the exercise with the other leg.

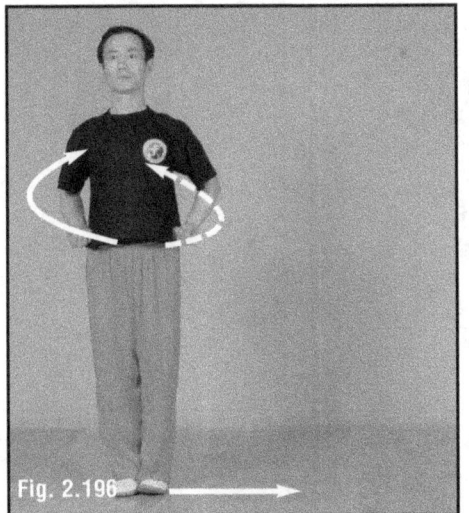

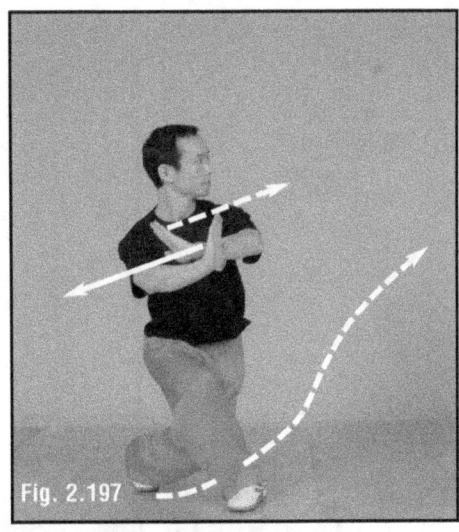

Special Tips: The force should be applied on the heel or the whole sole of the foot, not on the outer edge of the foot. Foot of supporting leg should be flat on the ground.

Front Sweeping Kick (Qian Sao Tui)

Stand sideways and assume a left "T" stance, look to your right (Fig. 2.199). Open your left leg to the left (Fig. 2.200) and immediately turn your waist counter clockwise and take a step obliquely left with the left foot (Fig. 2.201). Bend the left leg to a full squat lifting the heel from the ground. Use the ball of the left foot as an axis and straighten the right leg, toes inward and sole on the ground, then swing your arms naturally and execute the sweep until you complete the desired rotation (Fig. 2.202 to Fig. 2.03). To end the sweep, assume a right drop stance flashing left palm over your head and extending your right arm back into a hook hand with the fingers pointing up (Fig. 2.204). Look to the front.

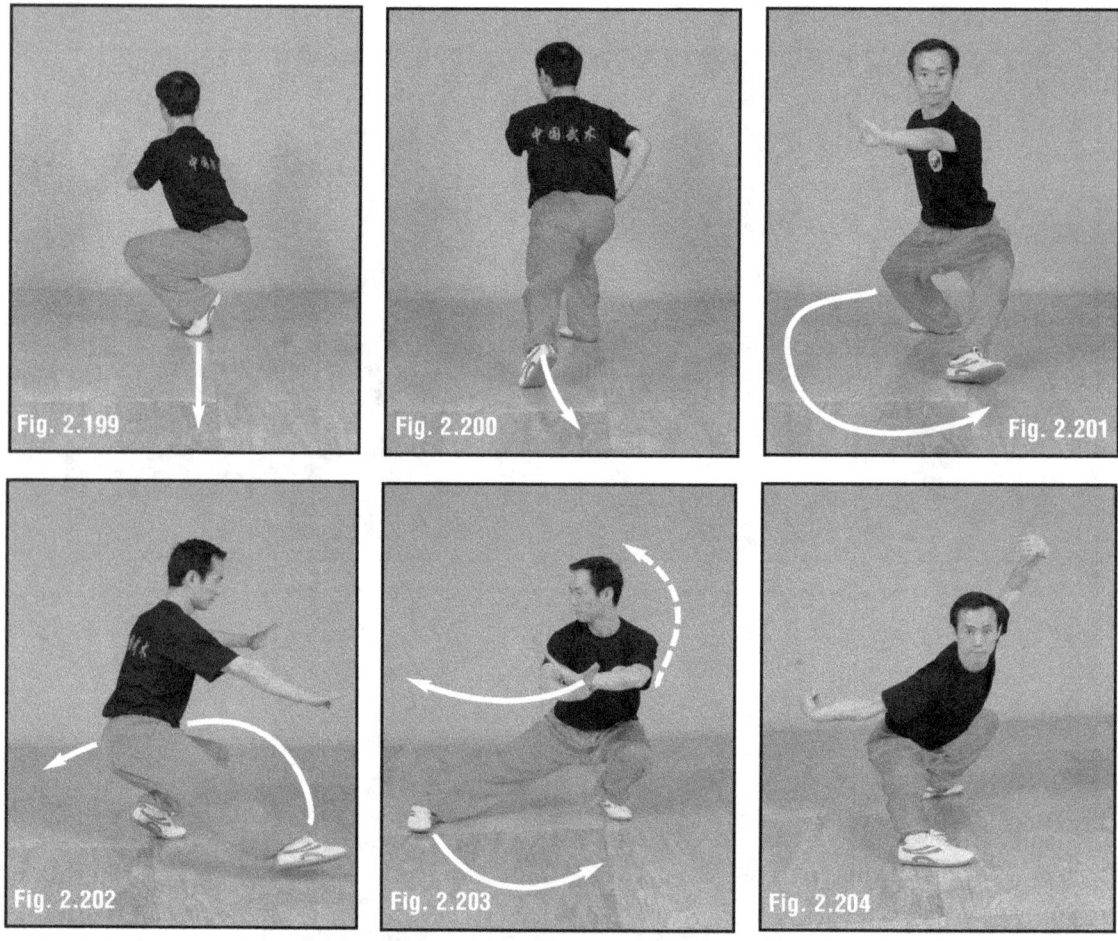

Special Tips: Keep your body upright and the chest out. The right foot must be flat on the ground and scratch it all the way through the sweep.

Back Sweeping Kick (Hou Sao Tui)

Assume a left bow stance and execute a double pushing palm, look forward (Fig. 2.205). After a short pause, swing both arms to your left (Fig. 2.206) and follow with a swift turn of your waist clockwise bending the left leg to a full squat, lifting the heel from the ground and turning the toes inward to initiate the sweep (Fig. 2.207). Using the momentum of the previous move and the ball of the left foot as the axis, complete the rotation desired (Fig. 2.208). To end the sweep, assume a left bow stance with your left palm pushing forward and your right arm extended behind your body in a hook hand with the fingers pointing down. Look forward (Fig. 2.209).

Fig. 2.205

Fig. 2.206

Fig. 2.207

Fig. 2.208

Fig. 2.209

Special Tips: Keep your body upright and the chest out. The right foot must be flat on the ground and scratch it all the way through the sweep. Alternately, the back sweeping kick can end in a right drop stance looking back depending on your specific routine.

2.5. Basic Combinations

The basic combinations of Wushu consist of a series of skills that are practiced together as single movements. For example, take a thread palm in drop stance; it is a sequence that allows the practitioner to integrate footwork, hand technique and a stance all together. In addition, the basic combinations include exercises that are not covered on other sections of the basic skills, such as the single body turn, which are common elements of routines that require consistent practice. On this section we have included five of the most common basic combinations and as you progress through them there are many variations that can be added.

Beginners should start by practicing the basic combinations recommended on this book step by step. The basic combinations are great to condition different body parts like the waist and lower back. The progress should be slow, especially since the correct execution methods and the inherent rhythms of each movement take time to grasp. But once mastered, they must be executed quickly and effortlessly. There are many possible sets of basic combinations since they integrate most of the hand techniques, leg techniques, stances and footwork of Wushu.

As you make progress in Wushu, you may be able to select basic combinations that are part of the routines that you usually practice and include them into your daily training program.

Straight Punch Front Snap Kick (Tan Tui Chong Quan)

Stand with feet shoulder-width apart with your hands as fists with the palms facing up and pressed against the sides at waist level. Take a half step forward with your left foot and place only the toes on the ground, at the same time, thrust your right fist out in a straight line, twisting the forearm inward just before impact so that the fist is facing down (Fig. 2.210). Perform simultaneously a straight punch with the left arm and a front snap kick with the right leg (Fig. 2.211). Hold the position for one second and perform simultaneously a straight punch with the right arm and a front snap kick with the left leg (Fig. 2.212). Hold the position for one second and perform simultaneously a straight punch with the left arm and a front snap kick with the right leg (Fig. 2.213). Hold the position for one second.

Special Tips: Keep your body upright and the chest out. Force should be applied on the face of the fist and the instep of the foot each time. Keep a good rhythm as you alternate from side to side, do not rush.

Push Palm Front Heel Kick (Deng Tui Tui Zhang)

Stand with feet shoulder-width apart with your hands as palms with the fingers pointing down and pressed against the sides at waist level. Take a half step forward with your left foot and place only the toes on the ground, at the same time, thrust your right palm out in a straight line, twisting the forearm inward just before impact so that the fingers of the palm are pointing up (Fig. 2.214). Perform simultaneously a push palm with the left arm and a front heel kick with the right leg (Fig. 2.215). Hold the position for one second and perform simultaneously a push palm with the right arm and a front heel kick with the left leg (Fig. 2.216). Hold the position for one second and perform simultaneously a push palm with the left arm and a front heel kick with the right leg (Fig. 2.217). Hold the position for one second.

Special Tips: Keep your body upright and the chest out. Force should be applied on the outer edge of the palm and the heel of the foot each time. Keep a good rhythm as you alternate from side to side, do not rush.

Single Body Turn (Fan Yao)

Stand sideways with feet together and extend both arms with your right palm pushing to the front and your left palm pushing back. Look to your right (Fig 2.218). Swing your arms to the left (Fig 2.219) and perform a back crossed step with the left leg while you raise the right arm to the right side of the body and bend your left arm at the elbow and place the palm in front of the right chest (Fig 2.220). Swing both arms to the left until they are extended on a straight line, slightly bend your knees and perform a counter-clockwise body turn with your body pivoting on your feet without changing your position on the ground (Fig 2.221). As your body faces to the right you need to arch your back and look back (Fig 2.222). The rotation ends with the legs crossed again and arms extended to the side to add stability (Fig 2.223). Step forward with your right leg and assume a horse stance, bring both arms in front of the chest, right palm over left palm. Look in front of your palms (Fig 2.224). Stand up with feet together by moving your left leg to the left, extend both arms with your right palm pushing to the front and your left palm pushing back. Look to your right palm (Fig 2.225). Repeat the exercise in the opposite side.

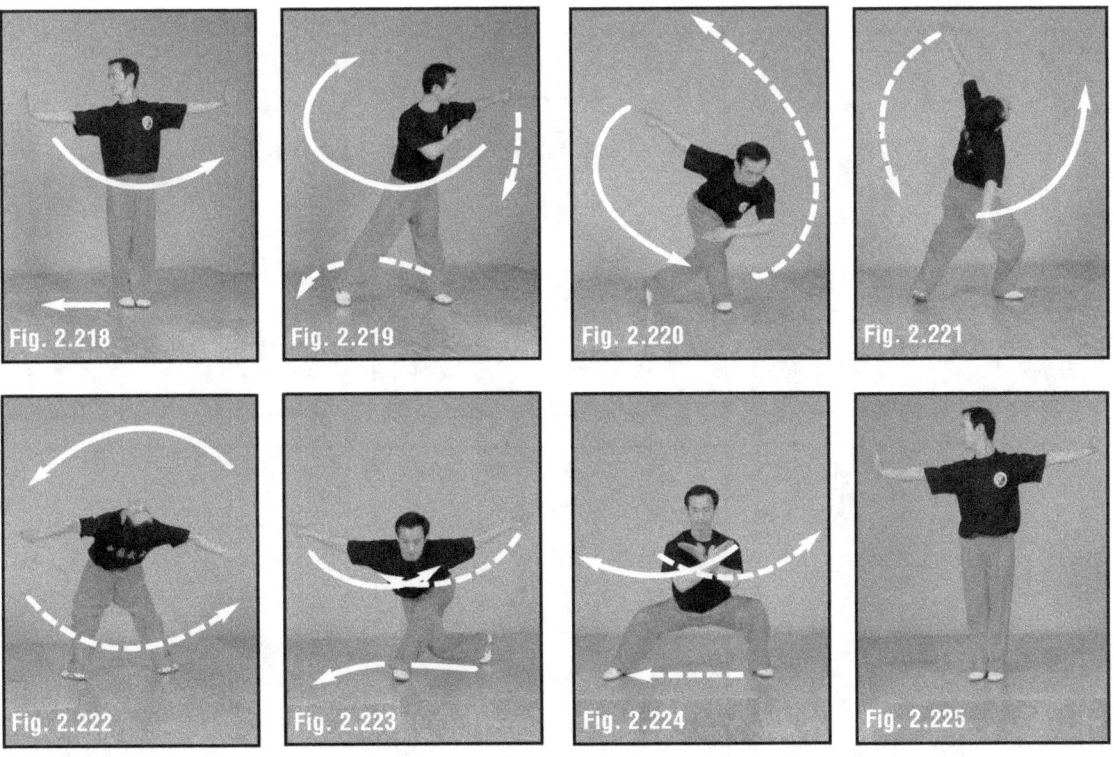

Special Tips: All movements should be performed in one single motion. Use the waist to guide the arms. Keep arms always straight. The pivoting motion should be quick and clean.

Mastering Wushu

Double Body Turn (Lun Bi Fan Shen)

As you walk forward with your right foot, thrust your right arm forward at shoulder level with the palm facing up. Look forward (Fig 2.226). Step forward with your left foot and thread your left palm facing up on top of your right arm, as you thread your body should bend forward and turn 90 degrees to the right with the right palm in front of the left armpit facing forward. Both knees are slightly bent. Look to your left (Fig 2.227). Perform a back crossed step with the right leg and turn your body another 90 degrees pivoting on the balls of your feet (Fig 2.228). Swing your right arm downward and upward in a circle until both arms are aligned (Fig 2.229). Continue to circle your arms, the right arms and waist without moving your feet from the same position (Fig 2.230 to Fig. 2.233). Stand on the right leg, pivot your body and make counter-clockwise 360 degrees turn while you bend the left leg by knee and hook it behind your right knee and swing both arms (Fig 2.234). As your body faces to the right you need to arch your back and look back (Fig 2.235). The rotation ends with the legs crossed again, step forward with your right leg and extend both arms with your right palm pushing to the front and your left palm pushing back. Look to your right palm (Fig 2.236).

Chapter 2

Fig. 2.232
Fig. 2.233
Fig. 2.234
Fig. 2.235
Fig. 2.236

Special Tips: All movements should be performed in one single motion. Use the waist to guide the arms. Keep arms always straight. The two pivoting motions should be quick, clean and continuous.

Thread Palm in Drop Stance (Pu Bu Chuan Zhang)

Stand with feet together with your hands as fists with the palms facing up and pressed against the sides at waist level (Fig. 2.237). Turn your body 90 degrees to the right and perform a back crossed step with your right leg towards your left and swing the left arm upward and to the right in a circle to press with your palm down in front of the right armpit, the right arm should be bent by the elbow with the fist pressed against the waist. Look to your left (Fig. 2.238). Bend the left leg at the knee and raise it while open your right fist into a palm and thrust it forward and upward, palm facing up, threading the back of your left palm (Fig. 2.239). Step with your left foot to the left and assume a left drop stance. Thread the left palm close to the inner side of the left leg forward and downward, and keep the right arm extended to the back in a straight line, both palms face to your right side with thumbs up. Eyes follow left palm (Fig. 2.240). Shift your weight from the right leg onto your left as you thread your left palm to assume a left bow stance, arms remain in the same position. Look to your left palm (Fig. 2.241). Repeat the exercise in the opposite direction.

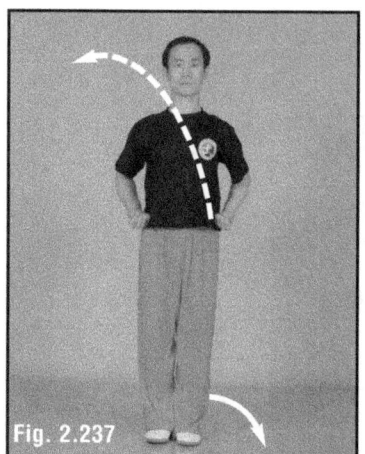

Special Tips: All movements should be performed in one single motion. Use the waist to guide the arms. Keep arms always straight and the body upright and chest out as you transition from drop stance to bow stance. Keep a good rhythm as you alternate from side to side, do not rush.

2.6. Balance Techniques

The Balance techniques of Wushu are comprised of a series of still stances on a single leg aimed to improve the ability to maintain bodily equilibrium. There are many different balance techniques depending on the position of the body (i.e. straight up, leaning forward, leaning sideways, leaning backwards), the position of the supporting leg (i.e. straight, in half squat, in full squat), and the position of the raised leg (i.e. straight, bent, pointing toes). On this section we have included six of the most practiced balance techniques and as you progress through them there are many variations that can be added.

Beginners may start by holding their balances anywhere from 10 to 30 seconds as their skill level improves. There are some easy ways you can improve your balance and stability. For balance, you can stand side to an object of at least waist height and perform a simple routine that progresses from knee bends to raised legs elevated to the front, the side and back. Lifting and lowering at various speeds with the legs straight or bent depending on which balance you are holding. For stability, you may practice your balances standing on a deep cushion or a balance board; this will strengthen your stability muscles in your back, hips, knees and ankles. Ankle weights can be used on the leg that is being raised to make the exercise even more demanding.

As you improve on your balance drills, you will gain firmness on you stances, footwork, sweeps and jump landings; which in turn will allow you to perform more advanced Wushu techniques safely.

Hooked Leg Half Squat (Kou Tui Ping Heng)

Perform a half squat with your right leg while you hook your left foot behind your right leg at knee level. Look to your right (Fig. 2.242).

Special Tips: Keep your back straight and chest out as you bend down. Arms position is optional depending on the specific movement performed with the balance.

Crossed Leg Half Squat (Pan Tui Ping Heng)

Fig. 2.242

Lift and cross your left leg over your right leg and place it slightly on top of your right knee, perform a half squat with your right leg. Look to your right (Fig. 2.243).

Special Tips: Keep your back straight and chest out as you bend down. Arms position is optional depending on the specific movement performed with the balance.

Raised Knee Balance (Ti Xi Ping Heng)

Shift all your weight to your right leg as you bend your left leg by the knee and raise it. Place your knee in front of the left side of your chest. Look forward (Fig. 2.244).

Fig. 2.243

Special Tips: Keep your back straight and chest out. The left foot should be aligned in front of the right knee with toes pointing down. Arms position is optional depending on the specific movement performed with the balance.

Fig. 2.244

Forward Balance (Yan Shi Ping Heng)

Stand on your right leg as you bend your left leg by the knee and raise it. Kick your left leg back and up behind you while you lean your body forward. Extend both arms to the side pushing out with the palms. Look forward (Fig. 2.245).

Special Tips: Keep your chest out, both legs straight and hips squared. Toes of the suspended leg should point back. Foot of supporting leg should be flat on the ground and optionally can be slightly turned inward for extra support.

Side Balance (Tan Hai Ping Heng)

Stand on your right leg as you bend your left leg by the knee and raise it. Open your hip and kick your left leg back and up behind you while you lean your body forward and sideways. Extend both arms with the right palm pointing forward and the left palm pointing to the back. Look forward (Fig. 2.246).

Special Tips: Keep your chest out and both legs straight. Toes of the suspended leg should point back. Foot of supporting leg should be flat on the ground and optionally can be slightly turned inward for extra support.

Hooked Leg Balance (Wo Yun Ping Heng)

Stand on your right leg as you bend your left leg by the knee and raise it. Bend your body forward and sideways, open your left hip and extend your left leg back and up behind you, hook your left leg back and to the right of your body. Arm position is optional depending on the specific movement performed with the balance. Raise your head and look to the right (Fig. 2.247).

Special Tips: Keep your chest out. Right leg should be straight. Toes of the suspended leg should be pointed. Foot of supporting leg should be flat on the ground and optionally can be slightly turned inward for extra support.

Fig. 2.245

Fig. 2.246

Fig. 2.247

2.7. Jumping Techniques

The jumping techniques of Wushu are perhaps one of the most distinctive aspects of Wushu amongst other martial arts. These movements require a proper approach run, a vigorous takeoff, a precise leg technique executed and completed in midair and a soft and an accurate landing. They are great for conditioning the legs and improving coordination and agility. On this section we have included six of the most practiced ones and as you progress through them there are many variations that can be added.

Beginners may starts by practicing low jumps first until their body becomes familiar with each movement. Basic requirements like jumping for height, jumping for distance, spinning in midair, etc. should be accomplished gradually. Every jumping session should include warm-up jumps such as running vertical jumps bringing one or both knees to the chest, running vertical jumps while arching your back and bringing both feet up to meet your head behind your back, running vertical spinning jumps to both directions, and more. The jumping front slap kick is the first jump technique to master, as it is included in most basic routines of Wushu.

As you make progress in Wushu, you will be required to jump anywhere between 20 to 40 times during a single practice session (professional athletes can jump more than 100 times) and when your body meets the ground is where the potential for damage is the highest. Understanding the mechanics involved on each jump reception is very important to avoid injuries. For instance, when practicing jumps that require body rotations, such as the jumping outside slap kick, make sure you jump for height first, then start and complete the spinning motion while still in midair. Hitting the ground while still twisting can be very dangerous for your ankles and knees. Once again, conditioning your leg muscles, tendons and ligaments is very important.

Jumping Front Slap Kick (Teng Kong Fei Jiao)

As you run forward (Fig. 2.248), step with your right foot forward and jump by kicking the left leg forward and upward, bringing your body as high as possible (Fig. 2.249). Then as you are in midair perform a front slap kick with your right leg slapping your right palm at the same time you bend your left leg at the knee and point the toes (Fig. 2.250).

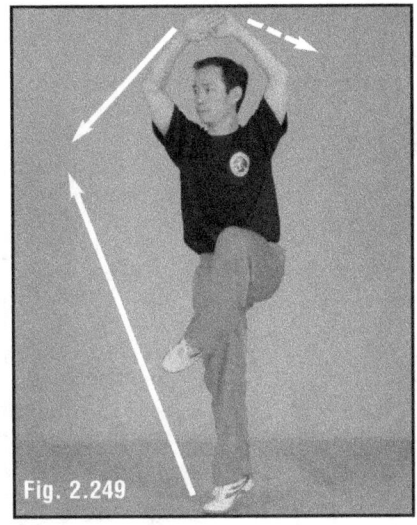

Special Tips: The kicking leg should reach shoulder level and the slap should be completed at the highest point of the kick. After the slap, the right leg should be brought down vigorously while you keep your chest out and body erect. You may land on your right foot, left foot or both feet depending on the technique that follows the kick.

Jumping Inside Slap Kick (Xuan Feng Jiao)

As you run forward, step with your left foot obliquely forward and immediately pivot on the ball of the left foot turning the body counter-clockwise 180 degrees and step forward with your right foot (Fig. 2.251). As you are about to place your right foot on the ground, shift the weight to your right leg and push off your right foot forcefully while swinging both arms simultaneously (Fig. 2.252). Bend the left leg and raise it to the upper left, perform and inside slap kick with your right leg (Fig. 2.253).

Fig. 2.251

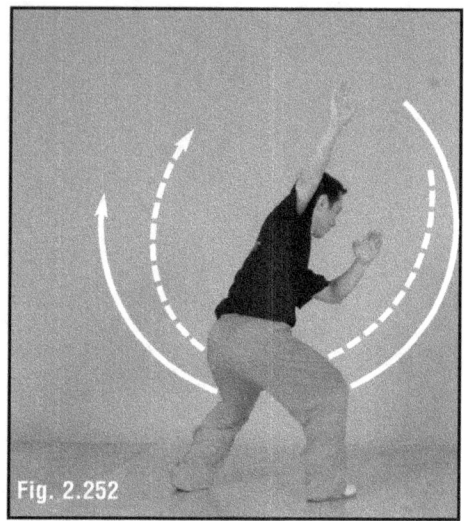

Fig. 2.252

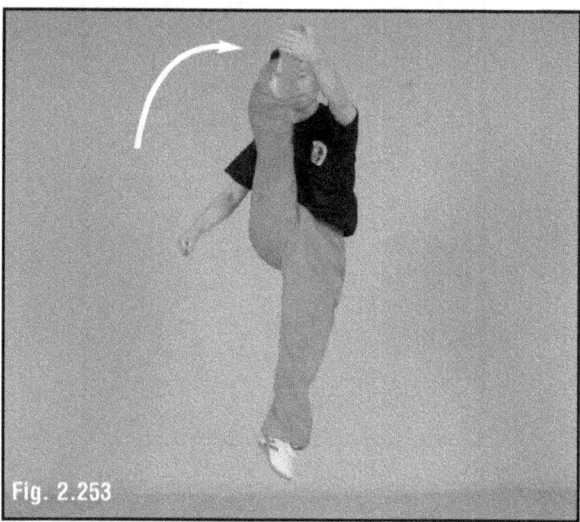

Fig. 2.253

Special Tips: The kicking leg is straight; the slap is made in front of the face. The left leg can be straight or tucked. The body should rotate no less than 270 degrees. The landing can be done on the right foot, both feet or on the left foot depending on the technique that will follows kick.

Chapter 2

Jumping Outside Slap Kick – Single Leg Takeoff
(Teng Kong Bai Lian – Dan Tui Qi Tiao)

As you run forward, step with your right foot obliquely right (Fig. 2.254). Swing your arms up and jump by kicking the leg left up and forward initiating a clockwise body rotation, bringing your body as high as possible (Fig. 2.255). Then as you are in midair perform an outside slap kick with your right foot (Fig. 2.256).

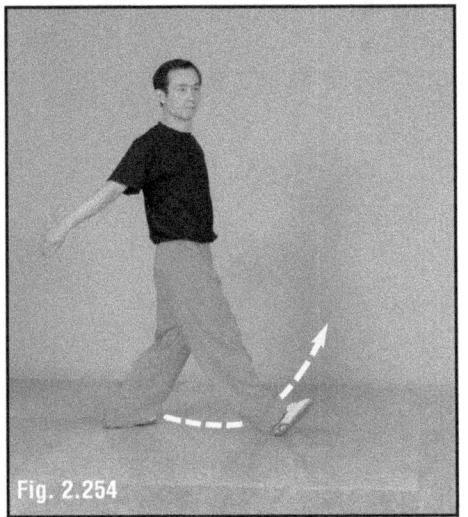

Special Tips: You may tuck in your left leg or leave it extended while in midair. The slap should be completed at the highest point of the kick. After the slap, the right leg should continue the outside swing while you keep your chest out and body erect. The body should rotate no less than 270 degrees. Landing should be performed simultaneously on both feet or on the kicking leg depending on the technique that follows the kick.

Jumping Outside Slap Kick – Double Leg Takeoff
(Teng Kong Bai Lian – Shuang Tui Qi Tiao)

Stand with feet shoulder-width apart, as you prepare to jump, you may swing your arms counter-clockwise while you perform a half-squat with both legs (Fig. 2.257). Swing your arms clockwise and jump forcefully upwards, let your arms, shoulders lead your body into a clockwise vertical twist (Fig. 2.258). As you turn, execute an outside slap kick with your right leg, slapping your left hand in front of your body at shoulder level (Fig. 2.259).

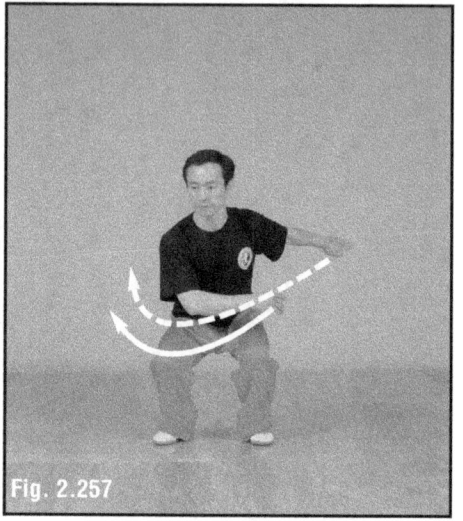

Fig. 2.257

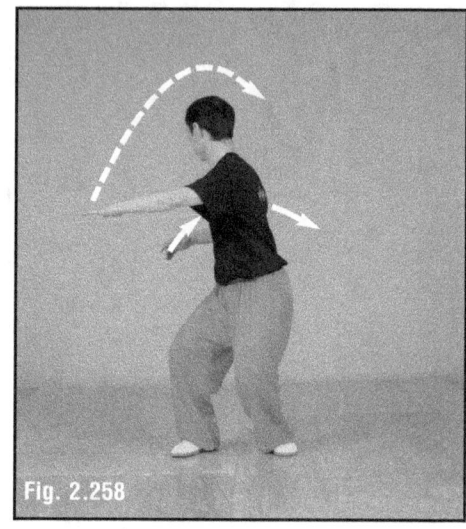

Fig. 2.258

Fig. 2.259

Special Tips: Use the momentum generated by the completion of the slap kick to continue to twist and prepare the landing according to the requirements. A variation of this jump starts with one or two single steps forward followed by a forward hop into the initial position described here.

Butterfly Kick (Xuan Zi)

As you run forward, execute a counter-clockwise body turn and quick hop backwards on your right leg. Begin to swing your arms in front of your body (Fig. 2.260). Assume a right bow stance and swing both arms and your upper body downward (Fig. 2.261), to the left and forward while switching your right bow stance into a horse stance (Fig. 2.262) first and later into a left bow stance right before takeoff. As your head comes up again and all your weight goes to your left leg, swing the right leg upward forcefully while the left leg straightens and pushes off from the ground (Fig. 2.263). Swing up your right straightened leg over horizontal level, toes pointed back, open your arms as far as possible raise your head and look forward (Fig. 2.264). Once the left leg goes over horizontal level the right leg drops, arch your back and let the left leg reach up as high as possible while the body continues to rotate with the back arched and the arms extended to the sides (Fig. 2.265).

Fig. 2.260
Fig. 2.261
Fig. 2.262
Fig. 2.263
Fig. 2.264
Fig. 2.265

Special Tips: Keep the chest out and the head up. Make use of the inertia of the initial body turn and hopping step to increase the height of your jump. The landing should be on your right foot assuming a right bow stance facing the direction that you were coming from.

Butterfly Twist (Xuan Zi Zhuan Ti)

As you run forward, execute a counter-clockwise body turn and quick hop backwards on your right leg. Begin to swing your arms in front of your body (Fig. 2.266). Assume a right bow stance and swing both arms and your upper body downward (Fig. 2.267), to the left and forward while switching your right bow stance into a horse stance (Fig. 2.268) first and later into a left bow stance right before takeoff. As your head comes up again and all your weight goes to your left leg, swing the right leg upward forcefully while the left leg straightens and pushes off from the ground (Fig. 2.269). Swing up your right straightened leg over horizontal level, toes pointed back, and immediately follow with your left leg, assuming a straight body position in midair. Bring your arms to the chest and begin a counter-clockwise twisting motion with the upper body (Fig. 2.270). The twisting action must be quick with the body aligned horizontally, the legs straight and toes always pointed (Fig. 2.271).

Fig. 2.266

Fig. 2.267

Fig. 2.268

Fig. 2.269

Fig. 2.270

Fig. 2.271

Fig 2.266   Fig 2.267 Fig 2.268 Fig 2.269   Fig 2.270 Fig 2.271

Special Tips: Keep the chest out and the head up. Make use of the inertia of the initial body turn and hopping step to increase the height of your jump. The landing can be done on the left foot, the right foot or both feet depending on the rotation desired and the technique that follows the jump.

2.8. Tumbling Techniques

The tumbling techniques of Wushu are comprised of a series of leaping, falling and acrobatic movements that are great for conditioning the body and improving coordination and agility. Most of these movements can be found as part of more advanced routines, especially in sparring sets as they represent actual attack and defense movements of Wushu. On this section we have included six of the most practiced ones and as you progress through them there are many variations that can be added.

Beginners may start by practicing tumbling techniques of Wushu on a safety mat and supervised by a qualified instructor at all times. For example, when learning how to fall, start from a low position and gradually increase the height and speed of the movement as you get a better understanding of the body mechanics involved. After diligent practice, your body will get stronger and used to absorbing the impact of the falls, allowing you to add any of these movements into your routines in order to enhance their degree of difficulty.

Lastly, is important to note that some of the tumbling techniques of Wushu, such as the front fall or the shoulder roll, can also be used to fall safely out of an over-rotated jump or any other unexpected landing to prevent possible injury. Having practiced falls can be advantageous on real fall situations.

Front Fall (Zai Bei)

Stand with feet together, body upright, bring both arms to the front of the chest, elbows bent with the outer side of the forearms facing front (Fig. 2.272). Close both hands into fists with the palms facing your chest. Keep your whole body straight, look to the left, lift your heels off the ground and let your body fall forward (Fig. 2.273). Maintain this position and land on both forearms bringing your chest as close to the ground as possible. Look to the floor (Fig. 2.274).

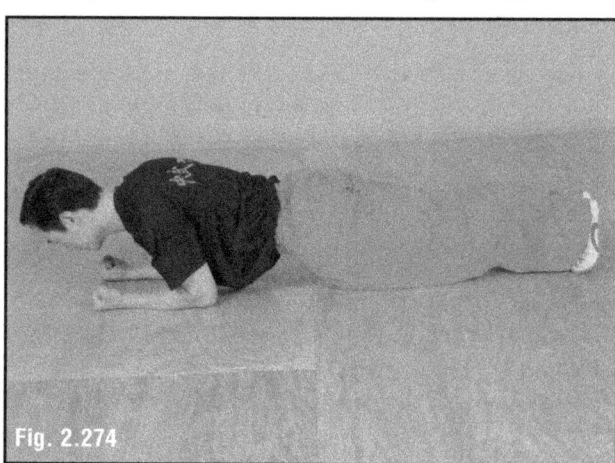

Fig. 2.273   Fig. 2.273   Fig. 2.274

Special Tips: Absorb the impact with your forearms and upper body. Alternately, both punches can be open into palms. Exhale through the nose as you hit the ground.

Shoulder Roll (Qian Bei)

Stand with your right leg in front and left leg behind, left heel is off the ground (Fig. 2.275). Bend your body forward and tuck your chin in. Slightly push off with your back leg and bring your right forearm in front of the body (Fig. 2.276). Roll on the ground starting from the leading forearm, then shoulder and through your back (Fig. 2.277). As you complete the roll, your legs should be in the same stance and orientation (Fig. 2.278).

Fig. 2.275   Fig. 2.276   Fig. 2.277   Fig. 2.278

Special Tips: Make your body like a ball and roll naturally. The roll should be performed on a small area, especially when combined to a weapon toss. Alternately, this movement can be performed after a leap forward.

Aerial Cartwheel (Ce Kong Fan)

As you run forward, make a hop on your right leg while you swing your left leg forward. Your right foot lands first and your left foot is placed forward assuming a high left bow stance. Lean your body forward and down while you bend both knees slightly (Fig. 2.279). Swing back and up your right leg forcefully and push off the left leg upwards (Fig. 2.280). Let your body rotate in midair along the same vertical plane, allowing your legs to continue over your body. Raise your head and chin, arms position is optional. Look to the ground (Fig. 2.281).

Fig. 2.279

Fig. 2.280

Fig. 2.281

Special Tips: The angle between the legs in flight should not be less than 90 degrees. Legs are always straight and toes pointed. The angle between the legs in flight should not be less than 90 degrees. The landing is your right foot first; end your body rotation naturally and place your left foot on the ground assuming a high right bow stance facing the direction that you came from.

Mastering Wushu

Jumping Inside Fall (Pan Tui Shuai)

As you run forward, step with your left foot obliquely forward and immediately pivot on the ball of the left foot turning the body counter-clockwise 180 degrees and step forward with your right foot (Fig. 2.282). As you are about to place your right foot on the ground, shift the weight to your right leg and push off your right foot forcefully while swinging both arms simultaneously (Fig. 2.283). Bend the left leg and swing it to the upper left, try to elevate your whole body horizontally and perform and inside kick with your right leg (Fig. 2.284). Tuck the left leg until the body finishes the rotation. Land simultaneously with the sole of the kicking leg, the left side of the left leg and both forearms and palms placed correctly in front of your chest area (Fig. 2.285).

Fig. 2.282

Fig. 2.83

Fig. 2.284

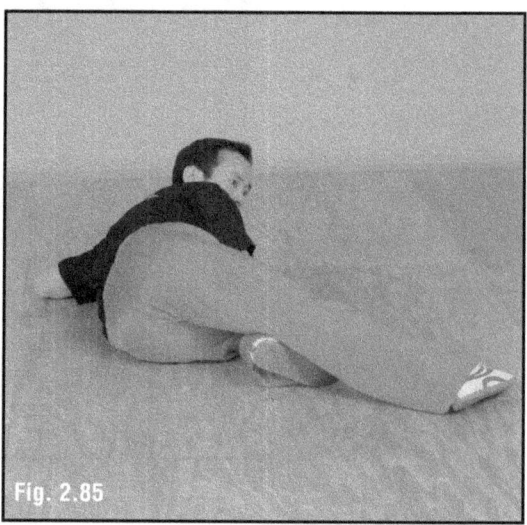

Fig. 2.85

Special Tips: The kicking leg should always be straight in midair, but it should be slightly bent when landing to avoid potential danger to the knee. The slap is optional.

Carp Skip Up (Li Yu Da Ting)

Start lying on your back. Bring both legs straight towards your head (Fig. 2.286). Place both hands on your thighs and push them upwards as fast as you can (Fig. 2.287). While your legs go up lift your body from the ground by pushing with your head (Fig. 2.288). Then at the highest point of the jump make a sudden change of directions with your legs meanwhile you bring your chest up. Land on both feet with your legs slightly bent and your back slightly arched until you are able to shift your weight forward and stand up straight again (Fig. 2.289).

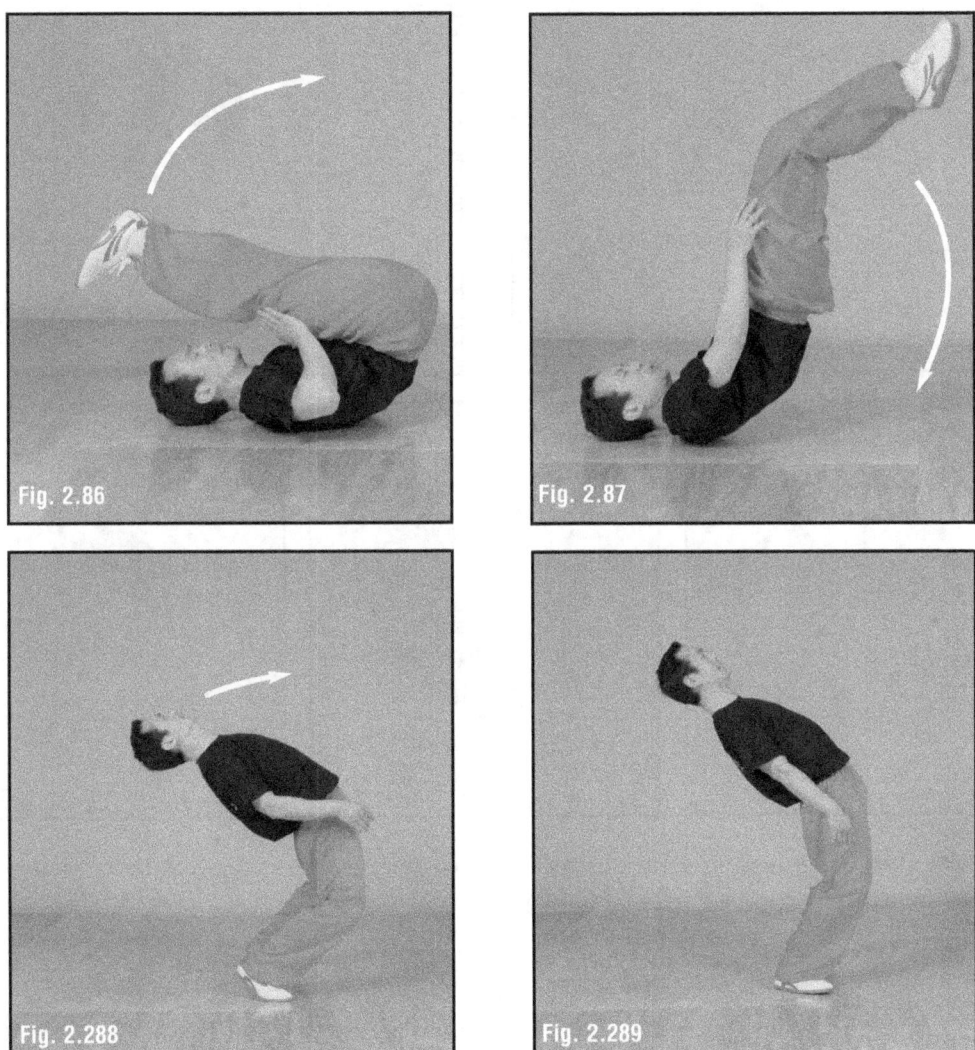

Fig. 2.86

Fig. 2.87

Fig. 2.288

Fig. 2.289

Special Tips: Pushing your legs with your arms, kicking your body up and turning over to land on your feet should be all executed in one single motion. Do not bend your legs on the initial movement. The landing should be done with your feet shoulder-width apart.

Dragon Coils Up (Wu Long Jiao Zhu)

Assume a side fall position on your left side (Fig. 2.290), swing your right leg in a counter-clockwise horizontal sweeping motion and follow with your left leg (Fig. 2.291). Lean your body backwards as your legs swing around (Fig. 2.292), shift the weight to your back and then to your shoulders (Fig. 2.293). Push off with both arms in order to raise your body upwards while the legs finish the last degrees of rotation. Place both feet on the floor and stand up (Fig. 2.294).

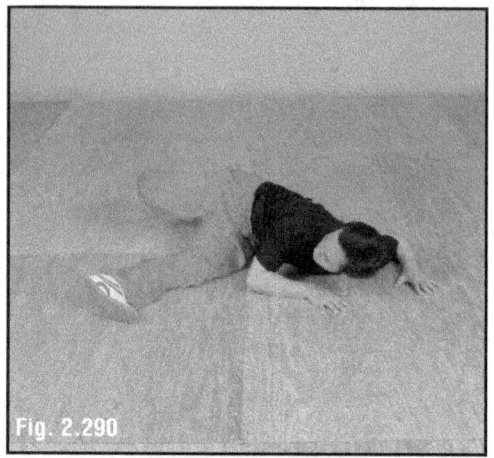

Fig. 2.290

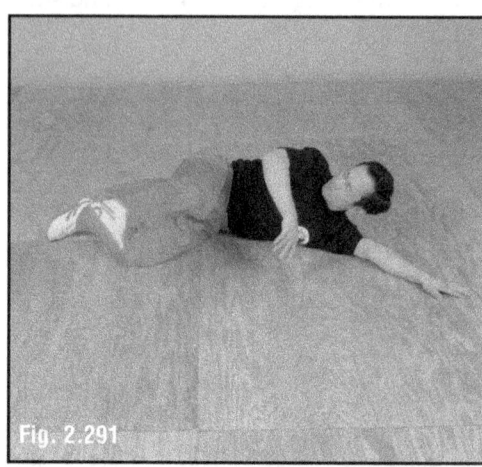

Fig. 2.291

Fig. 2.292

Fig. 2.293

Fig. 2.294

Special Tips: Keep legs straight and toes pointed during the scissor-like movement on the ground, use the momentum generated to help you raise your body up.

Chapter 3

Wushu Basic Routine

Mastering Wushu

The Wushu basic routine presented in this book is the Changquan Elementary Routine No. 3 (Chu Ji Chang Quan San Lu). This routine was compiled by the Chinese Wushu Association around 1960 as part of the standard curriculum of Modern Wushu. As the name indicates, it is the third routine of the program and it consists of 4 sections of 8 movements each, which explains why it is referred in some texts as the "32-Step Changquan". This routine is also known as the "3rd Duan Changquan" as it is a requirement for the 3rd Degree examination according to the ranking system implemented by the Chinese Wushu Association in 1997.

All major hand forms, hand techniques, stances, footwork, leg techniques, several basic combinations, two types of balances and one jumping technique of Changquan are included in this routine; providing an excellent way of practicing the basic movements learned during the first years of practice. Additionally, it is fair to say that this routine serves as a perfect introduction to Wushu competition as it is enforced in many national and international venues, such as the World Junior Wushu Championships and more.

This chapter contains step-by-step demonstrations by Jiang Bangjun covering every movement of the routine. Furthermore, in order to provide a more comprehensive description, the most complicated movements have been broken down into several steps and arrows have been added to the pictures to indicate the direction of arm and leg movements. Solid lines were used for the right limbs and dashed lines for the left ones. Definitions of typical Wushu terms such as "Straight Punch" or "Front Slap Kick" have been omitted since specific descriptions of these movements can be found in Chapter 2.

Lastly, the material presented here has been prepared to serve as a training aid or practical reference for our readers. In the event of having any slight difference with the official books compiled by the Chinese Wushu Association, the text of the official books shall prevail.

Wushu Basic Routine List of Movements:

Opening Movement
1. Opening Position
2. Flash Palm in Empty Stance
3. Show Fists in Ready Stance

Section One
1. Straight Punch in Bow Stance
2. Straight Punch Front Heel Kick
3. Straight Punch in Horse Stance
4. Straight Punch in Bow Stance
5. Straight Punch Front Heel Kick
6. Giant Leap and Swing Palm
7. Push Palm in Bow Stance
8. Raise Palm in Horse Stance

Section Two
1. Push Fist Down in Empty Stance
2. Lift Knee and Thread Palm
3. Thread Palm In Drop Stance
4. Up-swing Palms in Empty Stance
5. Push Palm in Horse Stance
6. Swing Palms in Back Crossed Step
7. Push Palm in Bow Stance
8. Turn Body Front Stretch Kick and Bending Elbow in Horse Stance

Section Three
1. Swing Arms and Hammer Fist in Resting Stance
2. Flash Palm in Drop Stance
3. Downward Fist in Bow Stance
4. Skip and Straight Punch in Bow Stance
5. Straight Punch in Horse Stance
6. Low Straight Punch in Bow Stance
7. Flash Palm in Back Crossed Step and Side Kick
8. Up-swing Fist in Empty Stance

Section Four
1. Pushing Elbow in Bow Stance
2. Turn Body and Front Slap Kick
3. Front Slap Kick
4. Jumping Front Slap Kick
5. Low Straight Punch in Resting Stance
6. Wheel Arms and Downward Fist in Drop Stance
7. Lift Knee and Uppercut Palm
8. Downward Chop and Straight Punch in Bow Stance

Closing movement
1. Flash Palm in Empty Stance
2. Show Fists in Ready Stance
3. Ending position

General Tips: This routine must be performed with clear and uniform rhythm, paying attention to the correct execution of each and every technique without rushing from movement to movement. The application of power should be smooth and accurate. The coordination of the eyes, hands, body and feet is important to properly display "consciousness" behind every technique. This routine shall not be performed in less than 1 minute.

Mastering Wushu

3.1. Opening Movement

1. Opening Position

Stand with feet together and arms straight with your hands pressed against the sides of your legs. Look to the front (Fig. 1.1).

2. Flash Palm in Empty Stance

Step diagonally back with right foot to form a left bow stance. Swing your right arm in a circle to the right and forward with palm facing up. Bring the left palm at waist level with palm facing up. Look to the right palm (Fig. 2.1). Shift your weight backwards onto your right leg. Raise your left palm and thread your right upper arm with both palms facing up. Thrust the left palm

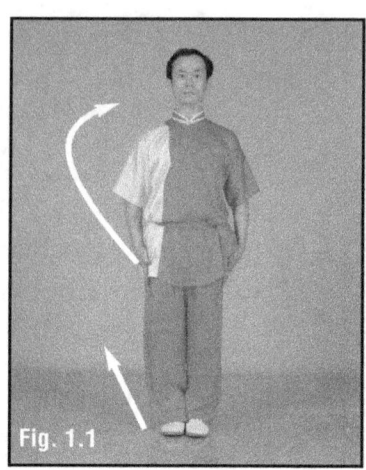

forward and bring the right palm at waist level with palm facing up. Look to the left palm (Fig. 2.2). Continue to shift your weight onto your right leg and assume a right empty stance. Right arm swings to the right and is raised up at the same time left arm moves down. Flash your right palm over your head, make a hook hand with your left hand with the fingers pointing up and look to the left, all at the same time (Fig. 2.3).

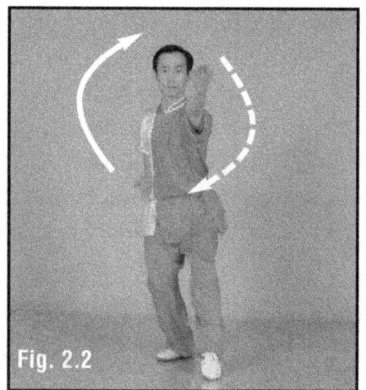
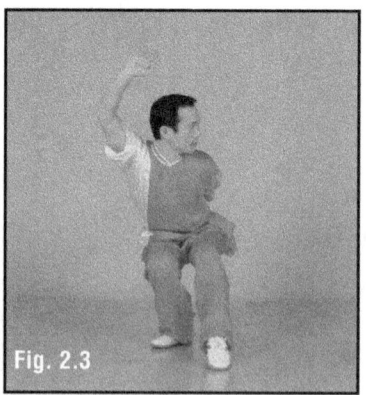

Chapter 3

3. Show Fists in Ready Stance

Stand up on your right leg and assume a left raised knee balance. Upper body remains in the same position (Fig. 3.1). Place your left foot front and shift your weight forward. Thrust both hands to the front with the palms facing up (Fig. 3.2). Step forward with your right foot. Swing both arms in a circle down and back (Fig. 3.3). Bring left foot forward and assume a ready stance with feet together. Swing both arms in a circle upwards (Fig. 3.4). Close both palms into fists and swing both arms down. Place both fist at waist level in front of the abdomen with palms facing down. Look to the left. (Fig. 3.5)

Fig. 3.1

Fig. 3.2

Fig. 3.3

Fig. 3.4

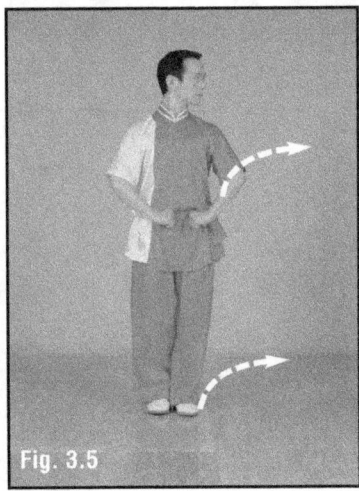
Fig. 3.5

3.2. Section One

1. Straight Punch in Bow Stance

Step to the left with your left foot and assume a left semi horse stance. Perform a left back hand block at shoulder height. Look to the left fist (Fig. 4.1). Turn your waist to the left and extend your right leg to assume a left bow stance. Perform a right straight vertical punch. Look to the right fist. (Fig. 4.2)

2. Straight Punch Front Heel Kick

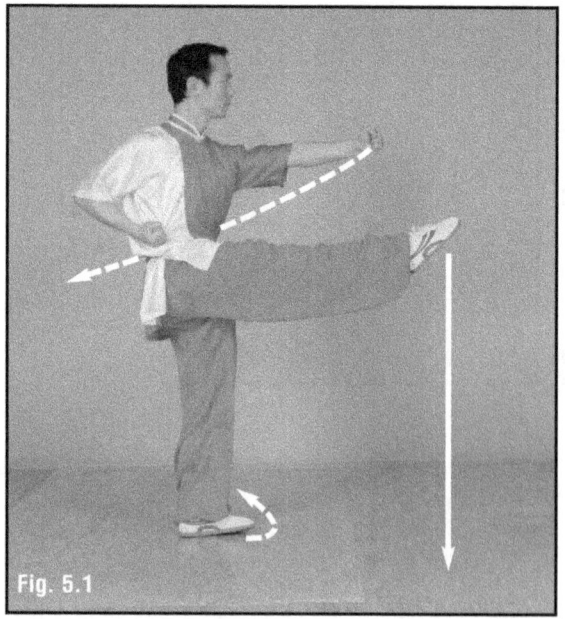

Shift your weight forward on your left leg and perform a right front snap kick and a left straight vertical punch at the same time. Look forward (Fig. 5.1).

3. Straight Punch in Horse Stance

Place right foot in front with toes turned inward. Turn your waist to the left and assume a horse stance. Perform a right straight vertical punch. Look to the right fist (Fig. 6.1).

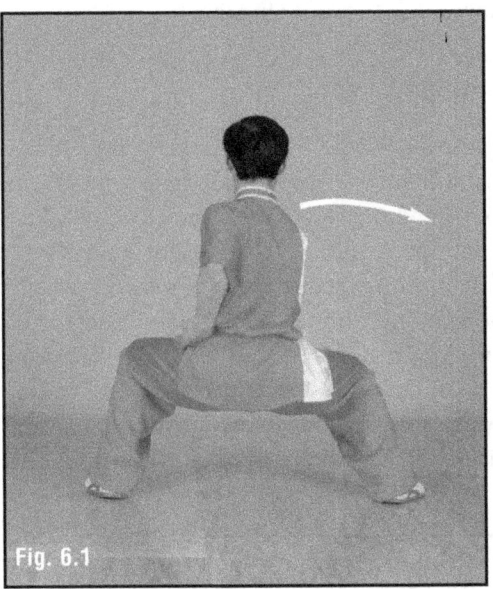

Fig. 6.1

Fig. 6.1 (Front View)

4. Straight Punch in Bow Stance

Step to the right with your right foot and assume a right semi horse stance. Perform a right back hand block at shoulder height. Look to the right fist (Fig. 7.1). Turn your waist to the right and extend your left leg to assume a right bow stance. Perform a left straight vertical punch. Look to the left fist. (Fig. 7.2)

Fig. 7.1

Fig. 7.2

Mastering Wushu

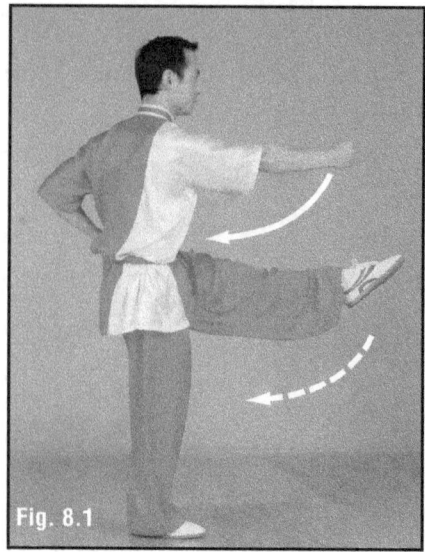
Fig. 8.1

5. Straight Punch Front Heel Kick

Shift your weight forward on your right leg and perform a left front snap kick and a right straight vertical punch at the same time. Look forward (Fig. 8.1).

Fig. 8.1

6. Giant Leap and Swing Palm

Bend the left leg at the knee and keep it raised. Open right fist into a palm and twist your right forearm inward touching your left knee with the inner side of your right arm. Palm faces down. Look to the right palm (Fig. 9.1). Place left foot in front of you as you shift your weight forward. Extend your left arm to the back and bring your right palm further back (Fig. 9.2). Jump forcefully with your left leg swinging your right arm forward and upward while turning the body the right and lifting your right knee. Eyes follow the right palm. As you are in midair, continue the natural circle with your arms so that the right arm presses back

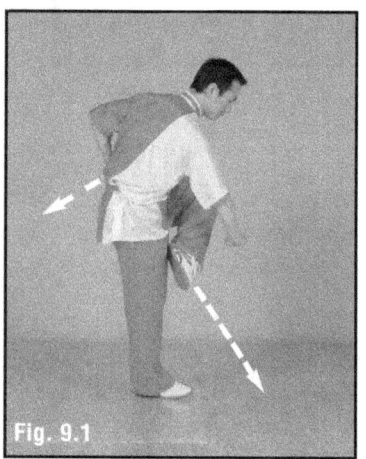
Fig. 9.1

Fig. 9.2

with the palm and your left arms presses up with the palm, the right leg is straight and the left is bent by the knee and pressed backwards with toes pointed (Fig. 9.3). Land with the right foot first and assume a left drop stance. Close your right palm into a fist and place it on the right side of the body at waist level. Swig left arm right and down and place palm in front of the right side of chest. Look to the left foot (Fig. 9.4).

Fig. 9.3

Fig. 9.4

7. Push Palm in Bow Stance

Sweep forward with left palm as you shift your weight forward from the left drop stance (Fig 10.1). Continue the sweeping movement of the left palm to the left and back, ending in a hook hand with fingers pointing up. Assume a left bow stance as you perform a right pushing palm. Look to the right palm (Fig. 10.2)

Fig. 10.1

Fig. 10.2

8. Raise Palm in Horse Stance

Thrust the left palm to the front threading over the top of the right underarm. Look to the left Palm (Fig. 11.1). Turn your left toes inward and center your body weight assuming a horse stance. Raise and flash your left palm over the head. Right palm remains in front of the left side of the chest. Look to the right (Fig. 11.2)

Fig. 11.1

Fig. 11.2

3.3. Section Two

1. Push Fist Down in Empty Stance

Shift your weight to your left leg and assume a right raised knee balance. Keep the left arm over the head and swing your right arm down and back ending in a hook hand with fingers pointing up. Look to the right hook hand (Fig. 12.1). Place the right foot down and assume a right empty stance. Close your left palm into a fist and push down with it on top of your left knee. Close your right hook hand into a fist and raise it above the head. Look left (Fig. 12.2).

Fig. 12.1

Fig. 12.2

2. Lift Knee and Thread Palm

Stand up and shift your weight to your right leg. Open both fists into palms. Right palm is pressed against the side at waist level facing up. Left palm is raised in an arc over the head and pressing down on the right side of the body (Fig. 13.1). Bend your left leg and assume a left raised knee balance. Thread your right palm over your left palm obliquely to the right. Right palm facing up and thrust delivered at eye level. Look to your right palm (Fig. 13.2).

Fig. 13.1

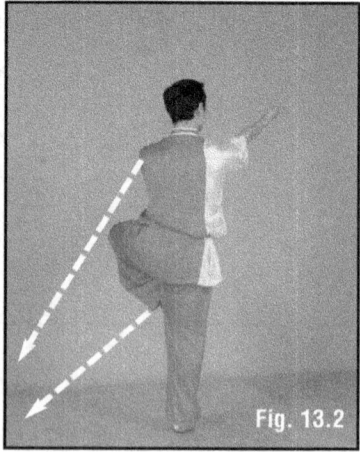
Fig. 13.2

3. Thread Palm In Drop Stance

Step obliquely left with your left foot and assume a left drop stance. Thread with your left palm on the inside of your left leg. The right palm remains extended to the back. Look to your left palm (Fig. 14.1). Shift your weight from your right leg to your left leg and assume a left bow stance. Arms remain extended (Fig. 14.2).

Fig. 14.1

Fig. 14.2

4. Up-swing Palms in Empty Stance

Step forward with your right foot, turn body 180 degrees counter-clockwise and assume a left empty stance. Swing the left palm up and backwards while you bring your right palm to the front at shoulder level. Up-swing both palms and look to the front at the same time (Fig. 15.1).

Fig. 15.1

5. Push Palm in Horse Stance

Stand up and shift your weight forward. Close your left palm into a fist and press it on your left side at waist level (Fig. 16.1). Perform a clockwise semi circle with your right palm and close it to a fist. Step forward with your left foot, turn your body 180 degrees clockwise and assume a horse stance. Press your right fist on your right side at waist level. Push with your left palm forward. Look to the left palm (Fig. 16.2)

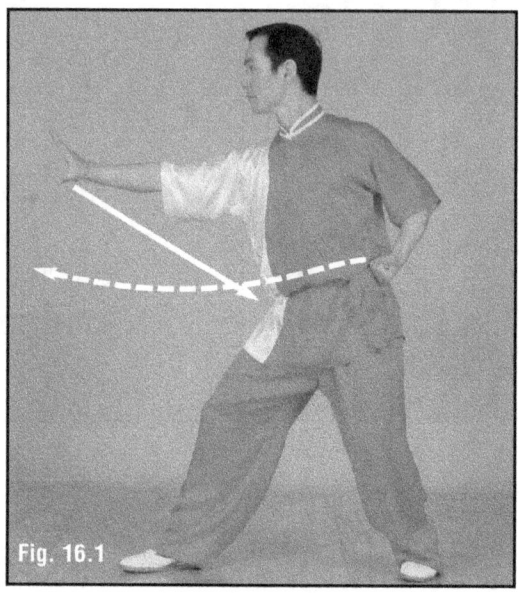

Fig. 16.1

Fig. 16.2

6. Swing Palms in Back Crossed Step

Swing both arms in an arc down and right. Look to the right. Perform a back crossed step to the left with your right foot behind your body. Swing both arms swing in an arc upwards and left stopping at horizontal position with palms upright. Look to the left (Fig. 17.1).

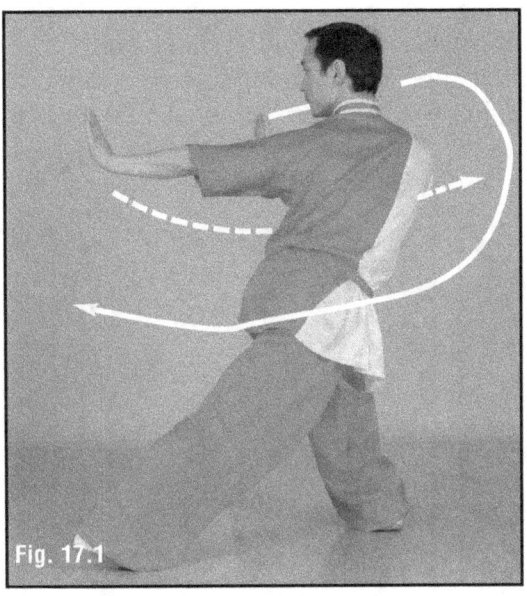

7. Push Palm in Bow Stance

Step back with your left foot and assume a right bow stance. Swing your right arm in an arc down and back ending in a hook hand with fingers pointing up. Push with your left palm to the front with palm upright. Look to the left palm (Fig. 18.1).

8. Turn Body Front Stretch Kick and Bending Elbow in Horse Stance

Open your right hook hand into a palm and swing right arm in an arc up to the front. At the same time, swing your left arm in an arc up and turn your body 180 degrees counter-clockwise, pivot on the balls of your feet (Fig. 19.1). Continue to swing both arms without moving your feet (Fig. 19.2). Continue to swing both arms, stopping left arm over the head and right arm on the right side of the body in a hook hand with fingers pointing up. Perform a front stretch kick with the right leg (Fig. 19.3). Place the right foot in front of you and press with your left palm in front of your chest. Close your right hook hand into a fist and press it on the side of your body at waist level (Fig. 19.4). Turn your waist 90 degrees counter-clockwise and assume a horse stance. Perform a bending elbow strike at chest level with your right arm. Look to the elbow (Fig. 19.5).

3.4. Section Three

1. Swing Arms and Hammer Fist in Resting Stance

Stand up from your horse stance slightly and open both arms to the side. Both hands are closed into fists with palms facing up (Fig. 20.1). Swing your right arm in an arc down and your left arm in an arc up. Turn your body 180 degrees clockwise pivoting on the balls of your feet (Fig. 20.2). Assume a right resting stance. Swing your left arm in an arc down and perform a hammer strike. Raise your right arm over your head. Keep both arms slightly bent by the elbow. Look to your left fist (Fig. 20.3).

Fig. 20.1

Fig. 20.2

Fig. 20.3

2. Flash Palm in Drop Stance

Open your right fist into a palm. Step forward with your left foot and turn your body 180 degrees clockwise to assume a right bow stance. Press left fist on the side of your body at waist level. Press down with your right palm in front of you at shoulder level. Look to the right palm (Fig. 21.1). Shift your weight back onto your left leg. Bend your right leg at the knee and raise it. Left fist opens into a palm and thread forward over the right palm (Fig. 21.2). Swing your right arm in an arc back and step back with the right foot and assume a left drop stance. Flash your right palm over the head and swing your left arm behind your body ending in hook hand with the fingers pointing up. Look to the left (Fig. 21.3).

3. Downward Fist in Bow Stance

Stand up on your right leg. Bring your left foot back and step obliquely forward in a circle. Open left hook hand and bring arm to the front of your chest in a sweeping motion with the thumb down. Right palm closes into a fist pressed on the side of your body at waist level. Look to the left palm (Fig. 22.1). Step with your right foot obliquely forward closing the circle to the left to assume a right bow stance. Perform a downward first with your right arm and strike your right forearm on your left palm in front of your chest. Look to the right fist (Fig. 22.2).

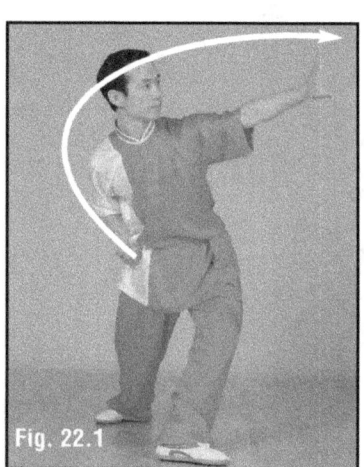

4. Skip and Straight Punch in Bow Stance

Rotate your body 90 degrees counter-clockwise and move your right leg back slightly. Shift weight on your left leg. Open right fist into a palm and keep your left palm hidden under your right armpit. Look at right palm (Fig. 23.1). Swing your right arm in an arc back on the left side of the body. Continue to swing your right arm up and down ending pressed on the side of your body at waist level. Swing your left arm in an arc left and up. Turn your body clockwise 90 degrees. Bend your right leg by the knee and raise it (Fig. 23.2). Press down with your left palm in front of your chest at the same time you stomp with your right foot and lift your left foot. Keep right knee a bit bent and slightly hook your left foot behind it. Body rotates 90 degrees clockwise (Fig. 23.3). Step forward with the left foot and assume a left bow stance. Perform a front vertical punch with your right arm. Keep your left palm hidden under your right armpit. Look to the front (Fig. 23.4).

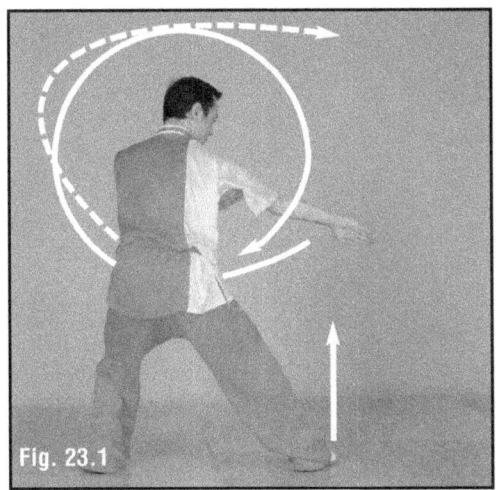
Fig. 23.1

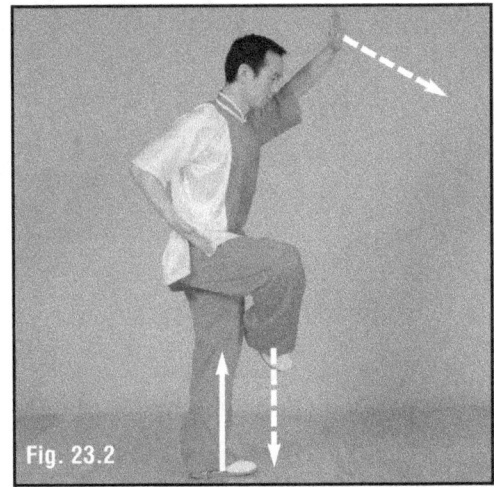
Fig. 23.2

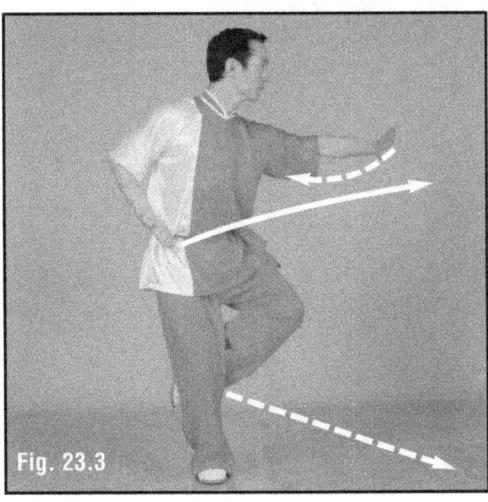
Fig. 23.3

Fig. 23.4

5. Straight Punch in Horse Stance

Rotate your body 90 degree clockwise. Assume a horse stance and perform a front vertical punch with the left arm to the left side of your body. Look at the left fist (Fig. 24.1).

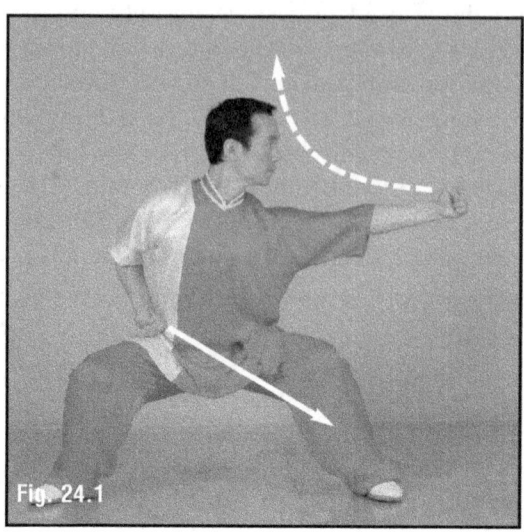

6. Low Straight Punch in Bow Stance

Cover your head with your left palm and rotate your body slightly counter-clockwise assuming a left bow stance. Perform a low straight punch with the right arm obliquely right. Look at your right punch (Fig. 25.1).

7. Flash Palm in Back Crossed Step and Side Kick

Stand up and perform a back crossed step with your right leg behind your body. Bring both arms in front of your chest, right palm over left palm. Look to the left (Fig. 26.1). Perform a side kick with your left leg while you raise your right arm over your head and swing your left arm back ending in a hook hand with the fingers pointing up. Look to the left foot (Fig. 26.2).

8. Up-swing Fist in Empty Stance

Place your left foot down on the left side of your body. Close both palms into fists (Fig. 27.1). Bend your right leg by the knee and raise it (Fig. 27.2). Rotate your body 180 degrees counterclockwise. Place your right foot in front of your body and assume a right empty stance. Swing your left arm back ending pressed on the side of your body at waist level. Perform an up-swinging fist with the right arm at shoulder level. Look to your right first (Fig. 27.3).

3.5. Section Four

1. Pushing Elbow in Bow Stance

Twist your right upper arm inward 180 degrees. Look at your right fist (Fig. 28.1). Jump forcefully with your left leg swinging your right arm in an arc up while turning the body the right and lifting your right knee. Eyes follow the right palm. As you are in midair, continue the natural circle with your arms so that the right arm presses back with the palm and your left arms presses up with the palm, the right leg is straight and the left is bent by the knee and pressed backwards with toes pointed (Fig. 28.2). Land with the right foot first and assume a horse stance. Bring your left arm in front of your chest. Look to your right side (Fig 28.3). Assume a left bow stance and perform a thrusting elbow strike with the left arm a shoulder level. Look to the front (Fig. 28.4).

Fig. 28.1

Fig. 28.2

Fig. 28.3

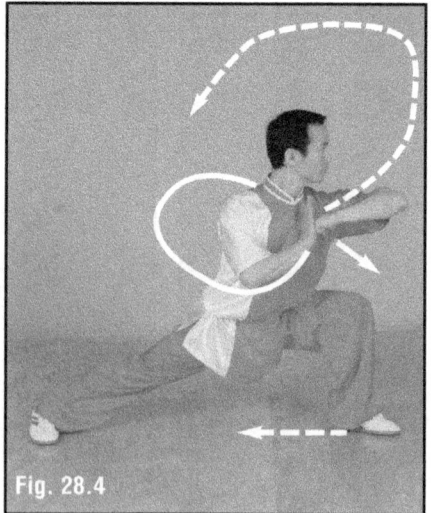
Fig. 28.4

2. Turn Body and Front Slap Kick

Step back with your left foot and center your body weight. Rotate your body 180 clockwise and extend both arms. Left arm extended to the front and right arm extended to the back (Fig 29.1). Perform a front slap kick with the left leg and slap it with your right palm. Press your left arm to the side of your body at waist level. Look to the front (Fig 29.2).

Fig. 29.1

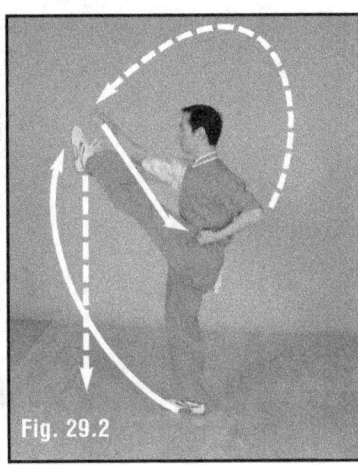
Fig. 29.2

3. Front Slap Kick

Place the left leg down in front of your body. Open the left fist into a palm and swing the left arm in an arc back, up and forward. Perform a front slap kick with the right leg and slap it with your left palm. Press your right arm to the side of your body at waist level. Look to the front (Fig 30.1).

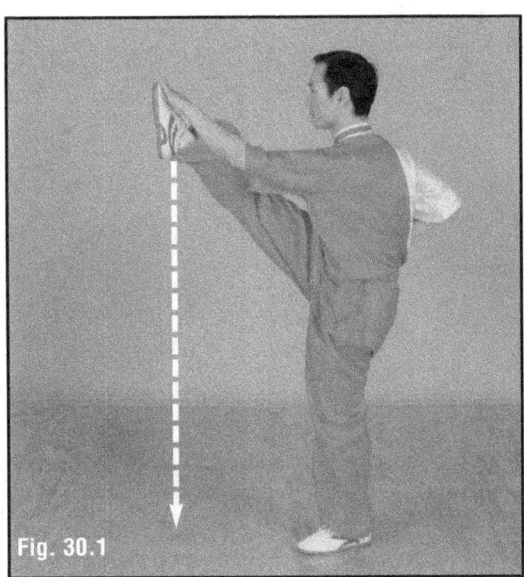
Fig. 30.1

4. Jumping Front Slap Kick

Place the right leg down in front of your body (Fig 31.1). Jump forcefully with your left leg and perform a jumping front slap kick with your right leg and slap it with your right palm. Extend left arm horizontally. Look to the front (Fig 31.2).

Fig. 31.1

Fig. 31.2

5. Low Straight Punch in Resting Stance

Land with the left foot first, then place the right foot in front of your body. Press down with your right palm in front of your chest. Press your left arm to the side of your body at waist level. Look to your right palm (Fig 32.1). Perform a clockwise semi circle with your right palm and close it to a fist. Rotate your body 90 degrees clockwise and cross your legs to assume a right resting stance. Perform a low straight punch with your left arm and press your right arm to the side of your body at waist level. Look to the left fist (Fig 32.2).

Fig. 32.1

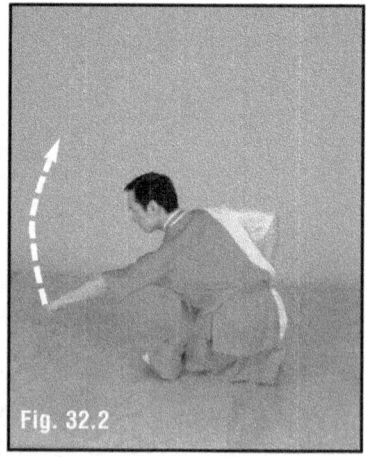
Fig. 32.2

6. Wheel Arms and Downward Fist in Drop Stance

Stand up and extend both arms. Left arm extended to the front and right arm extended to the back. Look to the front (Fig 33.1). Rotate your body 180 degrees counter-clockwise and swing both arms. Right arm swings up and left. Left arms swings down and right. Look to your left (Fig 33.2). As arms continue to swing, bend the left leg and assume a left raised knee balance. Look to the front (Fig 33.3). Step back with your left leg and assume a left drop stance. Perform a downward fist with your right arm on your right side over your right foot. Extend your left arm to your left. Look to your left (Fig 33.4).

Fig. 33.1

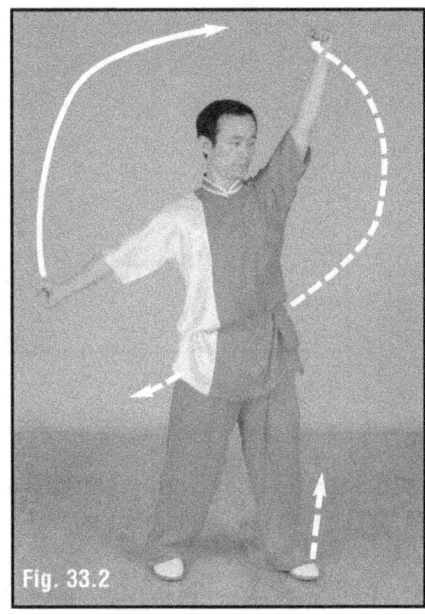
Fig. 33.2

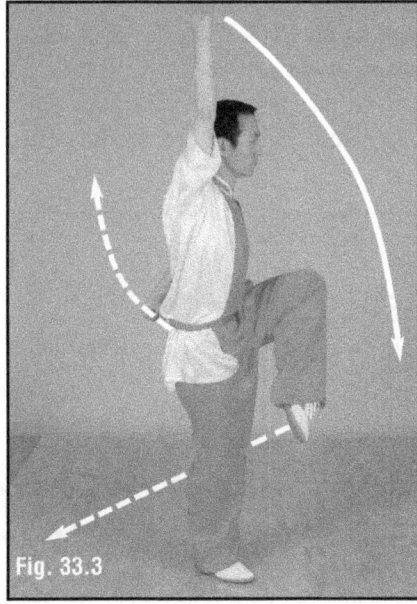
Fig. 33.3

Fig. 33.4

7. Lift Knee and Uppercut Palm

Open both fists into palms and shift your weight forward. Start to swing your arms in an arc. Right arm swings up and left arm swings down (Fig 34.1). Raise your right leg while your complete full vertical circles with your arms ending your right arm over your head and your left arm extended to the back in a hook hand with the fingers pointing up. Look to the front (Fig 34.2).

Fig. 34.1

Fig. 34.2

8. Downward Chop and Straight Punch in Bow Stance

Perform a downward chop with your right arm. Legs keep in the same position. Look to your right palm (Fig 35.1). Place your right leg backwards obliquely right and center your body weight. Swing your right arm to the right in front of your chest with the thumb down. Left palm close to a fist and is pressed to the side of your body at waist level. Look to your right palm (Fig 35.2). Perform a clockwise semi circle with your right palm and close it to a fist. Rotate your body 90 degrees clockwise and cross your legs to assume a right resting stance. Perform a front vertical punch with your left arm obliquely to the left and press your right arm to the side of your body at waist level (Fig 35.3).

Fig. 35.1

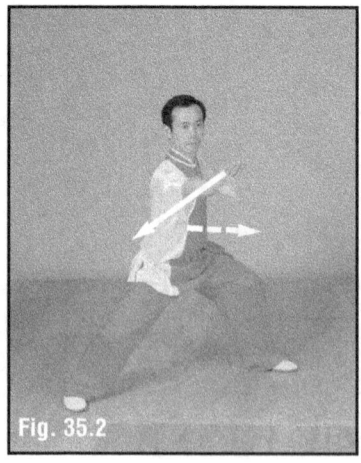
Fig. 35.2

Fig. 35.3

3.6. Closing movement
1. Flash Palm in Empty Stance

Raise your right leg and hook your right foot behind your left knee. Open both fists into palms and cross both arms in front of your chest. Right arm is over your left arm (Fig 36.1). Place your right foot backwards and bend the knee slightly. Shift your weight to the right leg while you swing both arms in an arc in front of your body. Right arm goes up, right and down. Left arm goes down, left and up. Arms end in front of your chest. Left arm is over your right arm Look to your left palm (Fig 36.2). Continue to shift your weight onto your right leg and assume a right empty stance. Right arm swings to the right and is raised up at the same time left arm moves down. Flash your right palm over your head, make a hook hand with your left hand with the fingers pointing up and look to the left, all at the same time (Fig 36.3).

Fig. 36.1

Fig. 36.2

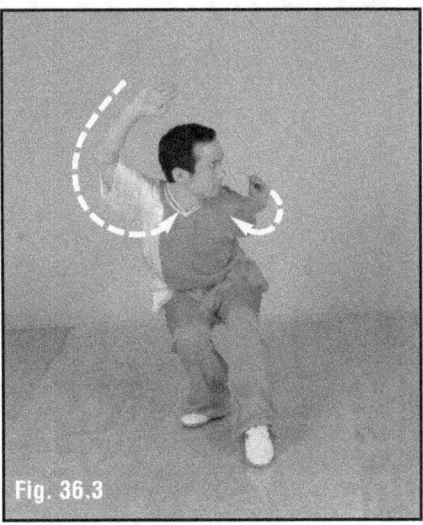
Fig. 36.3

2. Show Fists in Ready Stance

Stand up and step back with your left foot. Thrust both hands to the front with the palms facing up (Fig. 37.1). Step back with your right foot. Swing both arms in a circle down and back (Fig. 37.2). Continue to swing both arms in a circle upwards and downwards in front of the body. Close both palms into fists and swing both arms down. Place both fist at waist level in front of the abdomen with palms facing down. Look to the left. (Fig. 37.3)

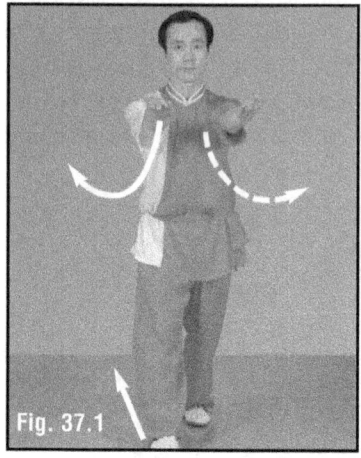

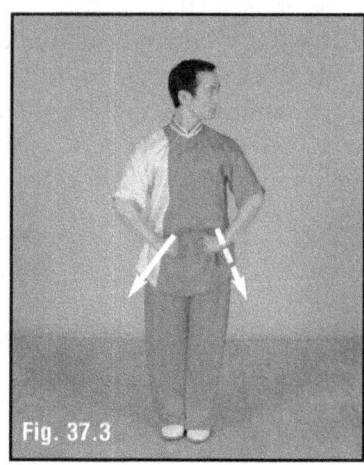

Fig. 37.1 Fig. 37.2 Fig. 37.3

3. Ending position

Stand with feet together and arms straight with your hands pressed against the sides of your legs. Look to the front. (Fig. 38.1)

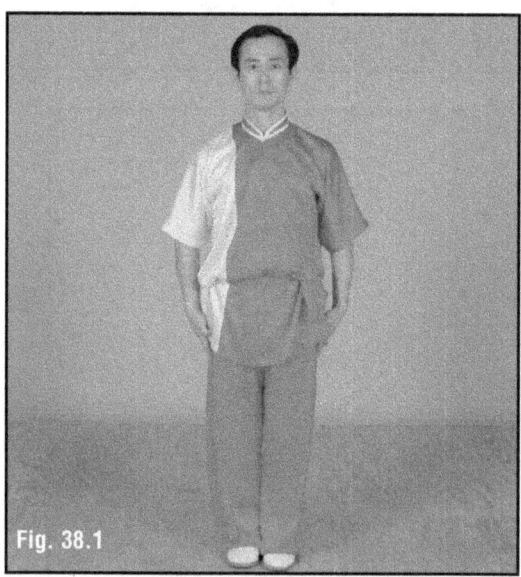

Fig. 38.1

BIBLIOGRAPHICAL REFERENCES

Chan, Anthony K. and Staples, Michael P. Wushu of China. Van Nuys. Delta Lithograph Company, 1978.

Cheng, Huikun. Chang Quan Quan Shu Ru Men (Basics of Long Fist Boxing). Beijing: Foreing Culture Publishing House, 1995.

Cheng, Huikun. Chang Quan Quan Shu Ti Gao Tao Lu (Advanced Routines of Long Fist Boxing). Beijing: Foreing Culture Publishing House, 1995.

Henning, Stanley. Ignorance, Legend and Taijiquan. Hawaii: Journal of the Chen Style Taijiquan Research Association of Hawaii 2 (3): 1–7. 1994.

Kang, Gewu. Spring Autumn: The Spring and Autumn of Chinese Martial Arts - 5000 Years -. Santa Cruz: Plum Publishing, 1995.

Kang, Gewu. Zhong Guo Wu Shu Shi Yong Da Quan (Chinese Wushu Complete Practical Guide). Taibei: Wuzhou Publishing House, 2003.

Li, Tianji and Du Xilian. A Guide to Chinese Martial Arts. Beijing: Foreign Language Publishing House, 1991.

Liang, Shou-Yu and Wu, Wen-Ching. Kung Fu Elements. East Providence: The Way of the Dragon Publishing, 2006.

Ma, Mingda. Shou Jian Cong Gao (Discourses on the Sword). Lanzhou: Lanzhou University Publishing House, 2000.

Mark, Bow Sim. Wu Shu Basic Training. Boston: Chinese Wushu Research Institute, 1981.

Several Authors. Wu Shu Ru Men (Foundation of Wushu). Zhejiang: Zhejiang People's Publishing House, 1983.

Several Authors. Zhong Guo Wu Shu Jing Hua (The Superior Chinese Wushu). Kowloon: People's Sports Publishing House, 1990.

Wu, Bin; Li, Xindong and Yu Gongbao. Zhong Guo Wu Shu Gai Yao (Essentials of Chinese Wushu). Beijing: Foreign Language Publishing House, 1992.

Wu, Victor. Changquan – Long Shadow Boxing. Hong Kong: Hai Feng Publishing Co., 1989.

ABOUT THE AUTHOR
Jiang Bangjun

Eagle Claw strength is based on fingers, hand and wrist power for effective gripping and locking.

Born in March 1971, Jiang Bangjun began practicing Wushu at a very young age. Raised in a family of Wushu traditions, his father was his first and strictest coach. In 1977, his family had to move from his native Chongqing to Renqiu, in the Hebei province. It is during this period that Jiang Bangjun's passion for Wushu started. Naturally active, after he entered the elementary school, his father used to wake him and his brothers up every morning to go jogging and to practice Wushu. So it is under the strong influence of his father that Jiang Bangjun went into the martial arts way.

In 1984, the young Jiang Bangjun was selected to be part of the North China Petroleum Sport Association Wushu Team. At that time, he was already one of the oldest team members, his way of practicing was very different and his joints were not so flexible. He knew that in order to catch up with the others he had to work harder, because like gymnastics, Wushu flexibility can be more easily acquired during the early youth. In June 1986, he placed 5th in Changquan (youth category) at the 7th Hebei Province Sports Meeting. This result is not worth to mention but it's at that time that he felt the excitement and motivation for further competition. In 1987, at the Hebei Province Wushu Championships, he placed first in Broadsword, second in Compulsory Empty hand, and fourth in Staff. Later that same year, Jiang Bangjun competed for the first time at the 6th National Sports Games in Guangzhou, the most premier sports event of China which is held every four years. This competition gave him the opportunity to broaden his ambitions and perspectives, and upon his arrival, he was accepted at the Daqing Sports Institute, in the Heilongjiang province. Training at the Daqing Sports Institute was extremely strict and strengthened all his Wushu foundation. During the weekends, instead of going home to see his family, he would remain with his coach who used to show him two very special videos he had, the 1987 adult and junior national championships, which he regarded as a treasure. Jiang Bangjun remembers watching those videos again and again; it was a great generation of insuperable champions, there was so much to learn.

Jumping high like an eagle watching its prey, Eagle Claw is spectacular to watch.

In 1989, Jiang Bangjun competed at the National Youth Wushu Championships winning two silver medals in Nanquan and Straight Sword. In 1990, he was admitted at the Shenyang Physical Education Institute in the Liaoning province. In 1991, he placed 4th in the National Wushu Championships in straight sword and continued to work upon his degree. In 1994, he helped the Liaoning Wushu Team to be promoted to the A division by placing 2nd in Straight Sword, 3rd in Eagle Claw and 4th in Sparring Sets. That same year, in July, he obtained a bachelor's degree from the Shenyang Physical Education Institute, immediately becoming a Wushu teacher at the same institution.

ABOUT THE AUTHORS

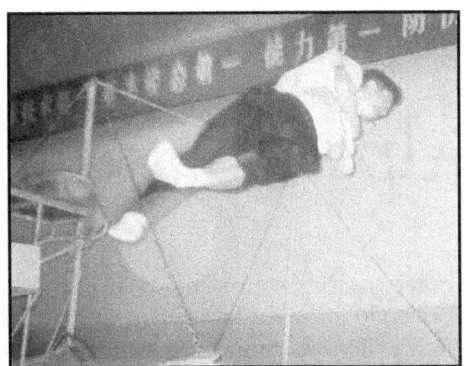

Never scared of the most grueling training sessions.

In 1995, famous coach Wu Bin invited Jiang Bangjun to join the Beijing Wushu Team, both as an athlete and a coach. Needless to say, the idea of being part of the very same team that Jet Li used to be part of was very exciting for him. During his childhood, the "Shaolin Temple" movies exerted a lot of influence on his passion for martial arts, and now he was also a Beijing Wushu Team member. And only one year later, in 1996, he enjoyed a very strong competition year thanks to his deep enthusiasm and consistent dedication. He won his first National All-Around title that year after his gold medals in Changquan, Straight Sword, Double Hooks and Sparring Sets, a major milestone of his career.

Unfortunately, Jiang Bangjun could not avoid suffering from the athlete's worst natural enemy – the sports injuries. As a result of the intense and voluminous training regimens used by elite Wushu athletes, he had severely damaged both of his knees. However, he was able to recover from his injuries and to make a remarkable comeback, winning for the second time the National All-Around Championship title in 1998. He then, continued to compete and to win several medals at national level competitions during 1999, same year that he was invited by the Hong Kong Wushu Association to be an Elite Team coach of the Hong Kong Wushu team, as part of their preparation for the 5th World Wushu Championships in 1999 and the 5th Asian Wushu Championships in 2000.

In 2000, Jiang Bangjun was selected by the International Wushu Federation as the official demonstrator for the new International Compulsory Routines of Changquan, appearing in the official instructional video, used also for the official books. In 2001, Jiang Bangjun concluded his official competition career with a gold medal in Changquan at the 6th World Wushu Championship in Armenia. After years of countless medals, 16 championship titles in Chinese National competitions, 2-time All China all-around titles and his World championship title, his competition career had finally reached an end. Nevertheless, he kept busy working as a coach both in China and abroad. For instance, in 2002, he was invited by the Russian Wushu Association to fly to Moscow to train the Russian Wushu Team for two months. Later, in 2003, he relocated to the United States where he currently resides. In 2004 and 2005, he was invited to by the President of the Confederation of Canadian Wushu Organizations to teach their national team in Toronto.

Due to his long list of national and international awards, including a "Wu Ying Ji" (Martial Hero Level) Athlete Certificate, an official Chinese Wushu 7th Degree and an International Athlete of Excellence Award, Jiang Bangjun is among the best qualified Wushu experts worldwide today. As an athlete, he combines the accuracy and perfection of the older generation with the athleticism, power and speed of the newer generation. As

During the 8th National Sports Games in Shanghai in 1997.

a coach, he has extensive teaching experience with groups and individuals of all levels, and his passion and commitment is incomparable. Currently, he shares his Wushu knowledge at his school, the Professional Martial Arts Academy, in Sterling, Virginia. He also keeps very busy organizing workshops around the country as well as taking full expeditions to China once a year.

ABOUT THE AUTHOR
Emilio Alpanseque

Changquan, with its fast movements, high jumps and cleanly defined stances is the backbone of Contemporary Wushu.

Born in 1967, Emilio began studying martial arts since the early 1980's. He practiced Taekwondo for several years and soon started to have an interest for Wushu being influenced by martial arts movie stars like Jackie Chan or Jet Li. He started to practice informally for recreation during the late 1980s, and watching two performances by the Chinese National Wushu Team in person was the crucial factor for him to switching over to Wushu indefinitely. However, his first real opportunity to receive formal training in Wushu did not happen until a few years later due to the lack of qualified coaches and good sources of information overseas.

In 1992, Emilio completed his college education in Computer Science and Management Information Systems and started his professional career as a software developer, two years later, his interest for Wushu took him all the way to China, where he was able to practice for the first time at the Beijing University of Physical Education and at the Shaolin Temple in Henan. Upon his return to Spain, he was sent on a business trip to Argentina where he had the opportunity to meet and practice with the 2-time all-around champion of China, Hu Jianqiang, and with the Shanghai Institute of Physical Education graduate Tian Shengping for a period of six months. Without a doubt, these experiences together were very significant, making him join the Spanish Wushu Research Institute in Madrid under the tutelage of Juan Carlos Serrato, one of the first generation Wushu Athletes of Spain, with a clear intention of becoming a Wushu competitor.

During his first year at the institute, Emilio practiced 5 to 6 days per week and got involved in the preparation of the Spanish National Team that was sent to the 3rd World Wushu Championships in Baltimore in 1995. He also started to learn Sanda with Zhou Lizhong, a China national champion and police forces trainer, in order to complement his Wushu knowledge in both areas. Two years later, he was already competing at regional level. Around that time, Emilio started to write articles about Wushu in the most respected martial arts and sports magazines in order to try to help the sport to become more popular.

Known as the "Father of all Weapons", the Staff sweeps all around as fast as heavy rainfall.

In 1997, Emilio ended up on the top positions of the Madrid Wushu Championships and earned the pass to compete at the Spanish National Championships for the first time. Having a silver medal in Sanda and one silver and two bronze medals in Taolu, he decided to compete in Taolu only, and his strategy paid off, being selected as part of the national Taolu team that was sent to the 4th World Wushu Championships in Rome, Italy. Without a doubt, Rome was a remarkable experience for him,

ABOUT THE AUTHORS

Known as the "Marshall of all Weapons", the Broadsword moves like a fierce tiger.

this was the first time he was exposed to an international Wushu event of this caliber, which opened his mind in all senses and made clear that there was a long way to go in terms of learning Wushu.

In 1998, Emilio continued to have the status of national team member and took his training to the National Institute of Physical Education. He also started teaching Wushu in a gym and at an elementary school. And later that year, he visited China again as part of the Spanish national team in order to practice in the Shanghai Institute of Physical Education and to compete at the 4th Shanghai International Wushu Festival, winning a bronze medal in the Broadsword event.

In 1999, Emilio enjoyed another strong competition season, however, mostly political and administrative problems kept him and other fellow athletes out of the final national squad that was being sent to the 5th World Wushu Championships in Hong Kong. This decision was very disappointing and forced them to device an alternative plan with a very short notice. They joined the Andorra National Wushu Federation and finally competed in Hong Kong representing Andorra. Needless to say, the whole experience was very stressful, but overall, it was another evidence of success against all odds. Once the competition was over, Emillio retired from official competition but remained in China that year and continues to visit periodically to persist on improving his Wushu knowledge at places like the Beijing University of Physical Education and at the Beijing Shichahai Sports Institute.

Already retired from competition but still training hard at the Beijing Sichahai Sports School in 2001.

In 2002, following a career opportunity, Emilio relocated to the United States, quickly becoming very active within the local Wushu community by training, coaching, judging and being a contributor writer to several international martial arts publications. He soon joined the Pacific Wushu Academy in Berkeley, California to train under coaches Zhang Hongmei and Phillip Wong. In 2003, Emilio won the Senior All-Around Champion at the 11th UC Berkeley Chinese Martial Arts Tournament. It was a way to remain active and motivated for training, especially during years of heavy loads of work that required him to constantly travel across the country and abroad.

In 2005, something that never occurred during his competitive years happened during a common practice session. He landed awkwardly from a jump tearing the anterior cruciate ligament (ACL) and damaging the medial collateral ligament (MCL) of his left knee. It was an unfortunate incident, but not something totally unexpected, Wushu is a high impact sport that entails certain room for injuries, especially on older practitioners and under uncontrolled conditions. Emilio underwent ACL reconstruction in December of 2005, followed by a year-long rehabilitation regimen, and in December of 2006 he was already back on the carpet during the opening demo at the 2nd East Coast Collegiate Wushu Tournament hosted by the University of Maryland.

Today, his extensive experience as a successful international competitor, former national team athlete, qualified judge and dedicated writer have made him a highly respected member of the international Wushu community.

Glossary of Terms

Aerial Cartwheel	侧空翻	Ce Kong Fan
Aerial Twist	侧空翻转体	Ce Kong Fan Zhuan Ti
Arm Rotations	臂绕环	Bi Rao Huan
Back Crossed Step	插步	Cha Bu
Back Leg Stretch	后压腿	Hou Ya Tui
Back Leg Swing	后摆腿	Hou Bai Tui
Back Sweeping Kick	后扫腿	Hou Sao Tui
Balances	平衡	Ping Heng
Bending Elbow	盘肘	Pan Zhou
Bow Stance	弓步	Gong Bu
Butterfly Kick	旋子	Xuan Zi
Butterfly Twist	旋子转体	Xuan Zi Zhuan Ti
Carp Skip-Up	鲤鱼打挺	Li Yu Da Ting
Cartwheel	手空翻	Shou Kong Fan
Crossed Leg Half Squat	盘腿平衡	Pan Tui Ping Heng
Double Body Turn	轮臂翻身	Lun Bi Fan Shen
Downward Chop	劈掌	Pi Zhang
Downward Fist	劈拳	Pi Quan
Dragon Coils Up	乌龙绞柱	Wu Long Jiao Zhu
Drop Stance	仆步	Pu Bu
Drop Stance Stretch	仆压	Pu Ya
Elbow Techniques	肘法	Zhou Fa
Empty Stance	虚步	Xu Bu
Fist	拳	Quan
Fist Techniques	拳法	Quan Fa
Flashing Palm	亮掌	Liang Zhang
Flying Step	跃步	Yue Bu
Footwork	步型	Bu Xing
Forward Balance	燕式平衡	Yan Shi Ping Heng
Forward Roll	抢背	Qian Bei
Forward Splits	竖叉	Shu Cha
Front Crossed Step	盖步	Gai Bu
Front Fall	栽碑	Zai Bei
Front Heel Kick	蹬腿	Deng Tui
Front Jumping Step	纵步	Zong Bu

Glossary of Terms

Front Leg Stretch	正压腿	Zheng Ya Tui
Front Leg Swing	正摆腿	Zheng Bai Tui
Front Slap Kick	单拍脚	Dan Pai Jiao
Front Snap Kick	弹腿	Dan Tui
Front Stretch Kick	正踢腿	Zheng Ti Tui
Front Sweeping Kick	前扫腿	Qian Sao Tui
Giant Leap And Swing Palm	大跃步前穿	Da Yue Bu Qian Chuan
Half Horse Stance	半马步	Ban Ma Bu
Hammer Fist	砸拳	Za Quan
Hand Forms	手型	Shou Xing
Hand Techniques	手法	Shou Fa
Hip Rotation	涮腰	Shuan Yao
Hook	勾	Gou
Hooked Leg Balance	卧云平衡	Wo Yun Ping Heng
Hooked Leg Half Squat	扣腿平衡	Kou Tui Ping Heng
Horse Stance	马步	Ma Bu
Inside Slap Kick	里合拍脚	Li He Pai Jiao
Inside Stretch Kick	里合腿	Li He Tui
Jumping Front Slap Kick	腾空飞脚	Teng Kong Fei Jiao
Jumping Front Stretch Kick	腾空正踢腿	Teng Kong Zheng Ti Tui
Jumping Inside Fall	盘腿摔/腾空盘腿	Pan Tui Shuai/ Teng Kong Pan Tui
Jumping Inside Kick	旋风脚	Xuan Feng Jiao
Jumping Outside Kick – Double Leg Take Off	腾空摆莲-双腿起跳	Teng Kong Bai Lian – Shuang Tui Qi Tiao
Jumping Outside Kick – Single Leg Take Off	腾空摆莲-单腿起跳	Teng Kong Bai Lian – Dan Tui Qi Tiao
Jumping Techniques	跳跃	Tiaoyue
Knee Bends And Rotations	膝部运动	Xi Bu Yun Dong
Kneeling Instep Stretch	跪压	Gui Ya
Leaning Ankle Stretch	压踝	Ya Huai
Leg Techniques	腿法	Tui Fa
Outside Slap Kick	外摆拍脚	Wai Bai Pai Jiao
Outside Stretch Kick	外摆腿	Wai Bai Tui
Overhead Fist	贯拳	Guan Quan
Palm	掌	Zhang
Palm Stretch	压掌	Ya Zhang
Palm Techniques	掌法	Zhang Fa
Push Palm Front Heel Kick	蹬腿推掌	Deng Tui Tui Zhang

Pushing Palm	推掌	Tui Zhang
Raised Knee Balance	提膝平衡	Ti Xi Ping Heng
Resting Stance	歇步	Xie Bu
Reverse Fist	横拳	Heng Quan
Shoulder Stretch	压肩	Ya Jian
Side Balance	探海平衡	Tan Hai Ping Heng
Side Fall	盘腿跌	Pan Tui Die
Side Kick	侧踹腿	Ce Chuai Tui
Side Leg Stretch	侧压腿	Ce Ya Tui
Side Leg Swing	侧摆腿	Ce Bai Tui
Side Splits	横叉	Heng Cha
Side Stretch Kick	侧踢腿	Ce Ti Tui
Single Body Turn	翻腰	Fan Yao
Single Butterfly Stance	单碟步	Dan Die Bu
Sitting Stance	坐盘	Zuo Pan
Sitting Stance Stretch	坐盘压腿	Zuo Pan Ya Tui
Splits Fall	跌竖叉	Die Shu Cha
Stances	步法	Bu Fa
Standing Splits	朝天蹬	Chao Tian Deng
Straight Punch	冲拳	Chong Quan
Straight Punch Front Snap Kick	弹腿冲拳	Tan Tui Chong Quan
Stretching Exercises	伸展活动	Shen Zhan Huo Dong
T Stance	丁步	Ding Bu
Tapping Step	击步	Ji Bu
Thread Palm In Drop Stance	仆步穿掌	Pu Bu Chuan Zhang
Threading Palm	穿掌	Chuan Zhang
Thrusting Elbow	顶肘	Ding Zhou
Tumbling Techniques	跌扑滚翻	Die Pu Gun Fan
Up-Swinging Palm	撩掌	Liao Zhang
Walking Step	行步	Xing Bu
Wheeling Arms	轮臂	Lun Bi
Wheeling Arms Slap Floor	乌龙盘打	Wu Long Pan Da
Wushu Basics	武术基本功	Wu Shu Ji Ben Gong

www.ingramcontent.com/pod-product-compliance
Lightning Source LLC
Chambersburg PA
CBHW081350080526
44588CB00016B/2439